Bank

for

KB175940

Business
Communication

dongyangb🙰ks

Benjamin McBride

Master's Degree in Education, University of Missouri

Bachelor's Degree in Philosophy, Cornell College

Eric J. Busch

Master's Degree in International Education, University of Alcalá

Graduate Certificate in TESOL, California State University San Bernardino

Bachelor's Degree in Spanish, Pennsylvania State University

Essential English for Business Communication

First published in October 2019

By dongyangbooks

22-gil 14, Dongyang bldg., Donggyoro, Mapo-Gu, Seoul, Korea

Publisher Kim Tae-woong

Editor Hwang Joon

Design Moon-C design

Price 14,000

ISBN 979-11-5768-547-9   13740

CIP CIP2019036548

www.dongyangbooks.com

Components Main Book / MP3

Essential English for Business Communication is the ideal course for students who aspire to succeed in the international business world. With English becoming increasingly prevalent as a lingua franca for international companies all over the globe, the demand for employees with high professional English competency has become an essential asset for driven business people who are non-native English speakers. This course is a perfect starting point for beginner-level English language learners to build a firm foundation of the vocabulary and expressions needed to function in the English-speaking business world.

Essential English for Business Communication is organized to gradually build learners' confidence in twelve common business communication contexts. Focusing on professional formal and informal business expressions, useful business vocabulary, and authentic situations, this course will first focus on the simple act of chatting with colleagues in a professional setting, followed by office technology discussion, the delegations of tasks in the office, telephoning skills, effective meeting language, and powerful presentation rhetoric. In the second half of the book, learners will discuss marketing, handle ordering supplies, practice negotiating, deal with money, gently complain and apologize, and correspond via email and letter writing. It is recommended that professors and learners follow the text in order from chapters 1-12 in order to progress in level of difficulty. With the completion of this course, learners will be prepared to communicate effectively in a wide variety of business English situations.

Each chapter consists of four main parts:

Key Expressions give learners 30-40 native expressions used every day in the English-speaking business world. This is the core of every chapter, as learners will use these expressions to complete a variety of realistic exercises.

Real Communication gives learners exposure to authentic-style dialogues, meetings, presentations, and emails to demonstrate how the key expressions are commonly used. Presented as listening practices, learners can solidify expressions in the proper contexts along with comprehension questions and summaries.

Try it Yourself gives learners an opportunity to utilize the key expressions and vocabulary for themselves in a guided but challenging activity. With many response options possible, learners can practice repeatedly in order to generate authentic usage of a variety of key expressions.

Reinforcement Review is an essential element to any comprehensive text-based EFL course. By practicing with a wide range of challenging activities that implement the key expressions, learners can even further reinforce what they've learned.

In addition:

Every chapter features an inviting warm-up activity to get learners started, useful "Real Business English" notes on expressions to give learners native-speaking insider knowledge, and a helpful answer key to wrap up the learning experience.

Table of Contents

Chapter	Key Expressions	Real Communication	Try it Yourself	Reinforcement Review
01 **Meeting New Colleagues**	How to talk about your job, department, company, and industry	Catching up with an old colleague and chatting at a conference	Use the key expressions to introduce yourself and chat about your position	Topical vocabulary and expression review plus a networking event dialogue
02 **Talking about Machines and Equipment**	Common expressions and vocabulary for discussing computers, printers, and other equipment	Using real tech vocabulary in authentic dialogues	Solve tech problems in the office with key expressions and vocabulary	A challenging vocabulary and expression review plus a tech issue dialogue
03 **Managing Schedules and Tasks**	Some of the most useful expressions for everyday English expressions	Realistic discussions about making plans and schedules	Practice making schedules and assigning roles	Review of the vocabulary and expressions and a dialogue about scheduling
04 **Talking on the Phone**	Useful expressions for difficult phone conversations in English	Challenging phone conversations including transfers and messages	Try talking on the phone yourself by using the key expressions	Specific telephoning expressions and vocabulary
05 **Business Meetings**	Meeting expressions for various delicate meeting situations	Chairing, expressing opinions, and interrupting in meeting dialogues	Implement real meeting expressions for speaking practice	Reinforcing meeting expressions and a full chair introduction
06 **Presentations**	Authentic presentation intro, body, and conclusion expressions	Listen to clips of a structured presentation using effective expressions	A real presentation monologue you can try yourself	Try again to present with native-speaker presentation expressions

Chapter	Key Expressions	Real Communication	Try it Yourself	Reinforcement Review
07 **Product Marketing**	Essential vocabulary to discuss marketing in English	Discussions on marketing, advertisement, and products	Discuss aspects of marketing with a colleague in an authentic conversation	Solidify your vocabulary in challenging practice activities
08 **Ordering and Supplying Goods and Services**	All of the necessary expressions for making and taking orders	Practice listening carefully to the specifics of ordering goods	Practice ordering with a colleague while utilizing the key expressions and vocabulary	A last look at all of the vocabulary and expressions for making orders
09 **Negotiating**	All of the expressions needed for every stage of a negotiation	Listen carefully to intense negotiations	Carefully implement new negotiating expressions	A second look at negotiating expressions and vocabulary
10 **Money Matters**	Vocabulary for money, trends and financial discussions	Dialogue discussions on changing figures and trends	Talk about money and trends yourself using new vocabulary and a graph	Increase your confidence by reviewing the difficult vocabulary
11 **Complaining and Apologizing**	All of the expressions needed for uncomfortable situations	An authentic listening with complaints and problems	Try delicately complaining to your colleague	Review the sensitive language needed to complain effectively
12 **Business Correspondence**	A comprehensive set of expressions to write professional correspondence	A special dictation listening practice using the key expressions	Complete emails using the key expressions	A final overview of both formal and informal emails

Essential
English for
Business
Communication

01
Meeting
New Colleagues

When meeting a new colleague, it is important to make a great first impression. This unit will give you the essential expressions and vocabulary to talk about your position, your company, and your industry.

Warm up

A **Match each question 1–3 with two responses a–f.**

1 What do you do?

2 What exactly do you do in your job?

3 What kind of company do you work for?

a I'm with Amtel; it's a multinational company.

b I'm an account executive.

c I work in the retail business.

d I'm responsible for planning the company's financial strategy.

e We manufacture sports equipment.

f I sell electrical products to wholesalers.

B **When you meet a new business contact, what do you say?**

manufacture	name	for	as	department

Hello, my 1_____ is Joon Choi, and I work in the electronics 2_____. I work 3_____ Dronix 4_____ an electrical engineer. We 5_____ custom computer parts for large companies.

Introductions and small talk

These expressions might seem familiar, but it is important to practice them so that you can use them naturally.

Hi, (name). How are you?

Hello, (name). Long time no see.

How's it going?

How are things with you?

How have you been?

Good to see you again.

(It's) nice to meet you.

How do you do?

It's a pleasure to meet you.

The pleasure is (all) mine.

Talking about your job/department

These expressions are useful when talking about your job.

What do you do?

What do you do for work?

- I'm an assistant manager.

- I sell car parts to foreign companies.

- I work at the national library.

- I work in the engineering department.

- I work as a marketer.

What is your job title?

- I'm an assistant manager of sales.

- I'm a technical director.

- I'm a lead engineer.

Do you work in an office?

- No, I work remotely.

- No, I work mostly from home.

Talking about your company

These expressions are useful when talking about your company.

Can you tell me about your company?

- We provide marketing services for retail stores.

- We provide tech solutions for companies.

- We are a multinational company.

- We are a relatively new company.

- We specialize in market research.

- We are known for creating innovative clothing products.

Talking about your industry

These expressions are useful when explaining which field your work in.

Which industry/field do you work in?

- I work in the tech field.

- I work in the accounting industry.

- I work in finance.

Sharing your contact information (business card)

These expressions can be used when sharing your business card.

Please take my card.
Here is my card.
May I have your card?
Let me give you my card.
Feel free to contact me anytime.

Quiz **Circle the best response.**

1   Hello, Jake. Long time no see!

   A Hello! How are things?   B It's nice to meet you.   C The pleasure is mine.

2   What do you do for work?

   A I work for an assistant manager.   B I am at city hall.   C I work for Secon as a designer.

3   Tell me about your company.

   A Please take my card.   B I work remotely.   C We provide accounting services.

4   What industry do you work in?

   A We are a multinational company.   B I work in the sales field.
   C I work as an account manager.

5   It was nice to meet you.

   A The pleasure is mine.   B How is it going?   C Hi, how are you?

Real Business English

Prepositions(in, at, for...) are essential when talking about your job, company, or field.
You should follow these patterns:

	e.g.	
I work **in + field, department**		I work **in the construction field.**
I work **at/for + company**		I work **in the accounting department.**
I work **as + job**		I work **at Amtek.**
		I work **for Amtek.**
		I work **as a stock broker.**

Listen to the dialogue below and fill in the blanks.

1

A Hi Barry, long time no see! How's it going?

B Jeremy, hi! Yes, it's been a while. I'm doing well. **1**_____ with you? I think you were working as an assistant the last time I saw you.

A Yeah, that's right. I actually moved to a new company. I'm working at Cardtop now.

B Oh, that's impressive! I've heard good things about Cardtop. **2**_____ there?

A I'm working as an account manager. I just have a few **3**_____ for now, but it's going really well.

B That's fantastic! I actually got out of the **4**_____.

A Is that right? What are you doing now?

B I'm working in marketing. It was a pretty big shift, but I'm getting the hang of it.

A That sounds interesting. My cousin is in marketing actually. Which company?

B Have you heard of Adslant? We're a relatively **5**_____. I'm working as a researcher there.

A Well, I hope you're liking it. I think marketing really suits you.

2

A Hi, are you here for the conference?

B Yes. I hope I'm not too early. The first speaker is at 9:00, right?

A Yes, that's right. Most people are still out in the lobby getting breakfast. My name is Kelly Stewart. It's a pleasure to meet you.

B **1**_____. I'm Tim Robbins. So what do you do, Ms. Stewart?

A Oh, you can call me Kelly. I work in the product development department at Metrice. What about you?

B I work for a **2**_____ as a coder. We design security solutions for app developers.

A That sounds really interesting! Where are you located?

A Our headquarters are in New York, but I work **3**_____. I live really close to here, actually, just a 10-minute drive.

A Well, that's convenient. You don't have to worry about hotels and transportation, I guess.

B Exactly. Was it a long flight for you?

A No, not too bad. My office is in San Jose. We **4**_____ yesterday, so I was able to get a decent night's sleep.

B Oh, it looks like they're getting ready to start. Let me give you my card.

A OK, great, and here's mine. Feel free to **5**_____ me anytime.

A Listen to the dialogues again and answer the following questions.

1 What is Jeremy's job title?

ⓐ assistant   ⓑ account manager

2 What field is Barry working in?

ⓐ finance   ⓑ marketing

3 What is Tim's job title?

ⓐ coder   ⓑ app developer

4 Why didn't Tim need to book a hotel?

ⓐ because he works remotely

ⓑ because his company headquarters is located nearby

B Summarize the dialogues.

> researcher   contact information   startup   account manager   assistant   remotely

In dialogue A, Barry and Jeremy are old friends who meet after a long time. Jeremy used to be an **1**_____, but now he's working for a new company as an **2**_____. Barry has left the finance industry and is now working in marketing as a **3**_____. His company, Adslant, is relatively new.

In dialogue B, Kelly and Tim meet at the start of a conference. They introduce themselves and talk about their jobs. Kelly works in the product development department, and Tim works as a coder for a **4**_____. Tim works **5**_____ and lives nearby, and Kelly took a plane from San Jose, where her company is located. They exchange **6**_____.

Don't forget !

Remember, in some countries people prefer to be called by their first names(Tim, Kelly...), but in some countries last names are more common(Mr. Robbins, Ms. Stewart...). If you are unsure what to call someone, don't be afraid to ask them!

Read what your colleague has to say and fill in the blanks with your own answers, using the hints on the side.

Practice A

Colleague	Hello! My name is Samantha Corbin. Nice to meet you.
You	1_____ ← Introduce yourself politely.
Colleague	Do you mind if I call you by your first name?
You	No, not at all. 2_____ ← Ask Samantha about her job.
Colleague	I work as an intern at Cortech.
You	Oh, I haven't heard of that company.
Colleague	We specialize in providing energy solutions for factories.
You	Oh, that sounds really interesting.
Colleague	What about you? What kind of work do you do?
You	3_____ ← Tell Samantha about your job.
Colleague	That sounds very interesting as well. Well, it was a pleasure meeting you.
You	The pleasure is all mine. 4_____ ← Offer Samantha your card.

Practice B

Colleague	Hi, there! Good to see you again!
You	Oh, hello Michael! 1_____ ← Ask Michael how things are going.
Colleague	I can't complain. What about you? I heard you're at a new company now.
You	Yes, that's right. 2_____ ← Tell Michael about your new company.
Colleague	That sounds really exciting! What do you do there?
You	3_____ ← Tell Michael about your new position.
Colleague	That's really great, congratulations. I'm late for a meeting. I'll talk to you soon.
You	OK, Michael, we'll catch up later.

A Fill in the blanks with the missing words.

field	solutions	department	contact

1 Here's my card. Feel free to _____ me anytime.

2 We provide security _____ for startup companies.

3 I work in the accounting _____ at a multi-national company.

4 I left the tech industry, and now I work in the education _____ .

B Choose the correct word(s) or the phrase to complete each sentence.

1 I don't have an office because I work _____ .
   ⓐ as a manager   ⓑ remotely   ⓒ in the finance industry

2 I work for Comtech. We _____ tech solutions for small companies.
   ⓐ provide   ⓑ give   ⓒ manufacture

3 I'd like to introduce my friend, Jason Williams. He works in the medical _____ .
   ⓐ field   ⓑ company   ⓒ director

C Choose the expressions from the box to complete the dialogue in order.

ⓐ It's a pleasure to meet you, too.
ⓑ We create insurance solutions for small companies like this one.
ⓒ Actually, I work in the accounting department.

A Excuse me. I'm here for a meeting. Do you work in this department?

B 1_____

A Oh, I see. Well, it's nice to meet you anyway. My name is Terrence Smithers.

B 2_____ I'm Catherine McNeil,
   but you can call me Cathy. You said you're here for a meeting?

A Right. I am supposed to meet with Francisco Munez.

B His office is on the second floor. Do you work here?

A No, I work for Fuller Medical. 3_____

B Oh, I see. Well, good luck in your meeting.

D Choose the correct words to complete each sentence.

1 It's a (nice/pleasure) to meet you.

2 We're an (established/old) company in the chemical industry.

3 I work (in/at) the purchasing department.

4 Kevin works (in/for) a startup downtown.

E Unscramble the words to make sentences.

1 started / industry / working / I / the / insurance / recently / in

→ _____

2 countries / to / export / companies / other / automotive / parts / in / we

→ _____

3 you / see / good / to / again

→ _____

4 works / ForumTech / for / as / he / researcher / a

→ _____

F Fill in the blanks with the given words from the box.

multinational	provide	card	department	pleasure

A Good morning. Are you here for the networking event?

B Yes, that's right. My name's Jason Lee. It's a **1**_____ to meet you.

A Nice to meet you, too. I'm Kimberly Plant. So what do you do, Jason?

B I am new to the pharmaceutical industry, actually. I was a nurse for 10 years, but I recently started working as a salesperson for a **2**_____ company based in New York.

A Oh, I'm from New York myself.

B Really? Where do you work?

A We are a small company, just a startup really. We **3**_____ research for some of the pharmaceutical companies in the area.

B Oh, that's very interesting. You are a researcher then?

A No, I work in the human resources **4**_____.

A I see. Can I give you my **5**_____?

B Yes, please. And here is mine. Again, it was nice meeting you.

A Likewise. Talk to you later.

02

Talking about Machines and Equipment

A modern office environment is centered around electronics and other machines. This unit will introduce vocabulary and expressions to help you discuss issues with computers, fax machines, printers, and other office equipment.

Warm up

A Match each question 1–3 with two responses a–f.

1 Why are you calling the IT department?

2 How can I fix this?

3 What supplies do you need?

a The printer is jammed.

b We are out of coffee in the break room.

c You should try rebooting your computer.

d You need to replace the ink cartridge.

e My computer is infected with a virus.

f We need two more chairs in the sales department.

B Your computer is not working right. How do you explain the problem?

version	technician	problem	connecting	infected

I'm having a **1**_____ with my computer. It's not **2**_____ to the internet.
I think it might be **3**_____ with a virus. I tried installing the newest **4**_____ of
the antivirus software, but it didn't work. I think I should call the IT **5**_____.

Talking about computer problems

These expressions will help you explain problems you are having with your computer.

What seems to be the problem?
- My computer is not working right.
- Something is wrong with my computer.
- My computer is not connecting to the internet.
- My computer is infected with a virus.

Are you having any difficulty with your computer?
- This software is not installing properly.
- I'm having problems adjusting the language settings.
- I can't open the file you sent me.
- The WIFI seems to be down.

Talking about computer solutions

These expressions are useful for fixing computer problems.

How can I fix the problem?
- You should try rebooting your computer.
- You should install the newest version of the operating system.
- Try resetting the router.

Why can't I open the file?
- You need to convert the file to PDF format.
- Please adjust the sharing permissions so that I can read the file.

Talking about printers and fax machine problems

These expressions will help you explain problems with printers and fax machines.

What seems to be the problem?
- The printer is jammed.
- The printer is out of ink.

What's wrong with the fax machine?
- I'm not able to send/receive a fax.
- The fax machine is offline.

Talking about printers and fax machine solutions

These expressions are useful for solving printer and fax machine problems.

How can I fix the problem?
- Try reconnecting the cable.
- You need to replace the ink cartridge.
- Try turning it off and back on again.
- We need to call the technician.

Making requests for equipment and supplies

These expressions will help you request additional supplies or items for office equipment.

We need more printer paper in the marketing department.

We are out of coffee in the break room.

We need three more desks in R&D.

Could you send an IT technician to the sales department?

Could you get a box of pens from the supply closet/cabinet?

Could you ask the office manager for an ink cartridge?

Quiz Circle the best response.

1 What's wrong with the printer?

   A I think it's stuck.   B I think it's jammed.   C I think it's stopped.

2 How do I fix the problem?

   A The software is not installing properly.   B Try reconnecting the cable.

   C I think it's infected with a virus.

3 What's wrong with the internet?

   A I think the WIFI is down.   B I think the WIFI is broken.   C I think the WIFI is jammed.

4 How can I fix this?

   A I can't open the file you sent me.   B The printer is out of ink.

   C You should call the IT technician.

5 What do you need?

   A You should try to reboot your computer.   B The office manager is out sick.

   C We're out of printer paper.

Real Business English

When you are helping someone to solve a technical problem ("troubleshooting"), it's common to use the verb "try." This verb should be followed by an -ing verb. Be careful, because **try + TO VERB** has a different meaning than **try + VERB-ING**.

I will **try to fix** the computer. = I will make an attempt to fix the computer

I will **try updating** the software. = Among the possible solutions, I will attempt this solution.

e.g.   Have you **tried reconnecting** the printer cable?

Have you tried to reconnect the printer cable?

You should **try rebooting** the computer.

You should try to reboot the computer.

Try converting the file to a different format.

Try to convert the file to a different format.

Listen to the dialogue below and fill in the blanks.

1

A   Hi, Janice. How are things with you?

B   Not so great, Kenny. Something is **1**_____ with my computer, I'm afraid.

A   What seems to be the problem?

B   I'm having problems adjusting the language **2**_____.

A   Oh, I see. I had the same problem last week, actually. Maybe I can help.

B   Oh, that would be great, thanks! How did you fix it?

A   Well, first, have you tried **3**_____ your computer?

B   Yes, I did that straight away, but it's still not working right.

A   OK, in that case you should **4**_____ the newest **5**_____ of the operating system.

B   Oh, is that the problem? Ok, I'll try that next. Thanks a lot, Kenny.

A   My pleasure. Let me know if it works!

2

A   Hello, this is Sharon in IT, how can I help you?

B   Hi, Sharon, this is Ray Stevens over in human resources. Can you send an IT **1**_____ to the HR department?

A   All of our technicians are busy at the moment. What seems to be the problem?

B   Well, the fax machine is **2**_____. It's rather urgent, I'm afraid.

A   Oh, I see. Maybe we can fix this over the phone. First, try turning the fax machine off and back on again. Sometimes that works.

B   OK, let me try that... No, it's still offline, unfortunately. Maybe the WIFI is **3**_____?

A   No, I don't think that's it. The fax machines are not connected to WIFI. Why don't you try reconnecting the **4**_____ that plugs into the back of the machine?

B   All right, I'll try that... Still no connection, I'm afraid.

A   OK. Look at the **5**_____ on the front. Do you see a green light there?

B   No, there's a blinking red light.

A   Oh, I see. We'll need to send the technician in that case. Can you wait until 11:30?

B   Yes, that's no problem. Thanks for your help, Sharon.

A   Listen to the dialogues again and answer the following questions.

1   What is the problem that Janice is having?
ⓐ adjusting the language settings   ⓑ installing an operating system

2   What solution has Janice already tried?
ⓐ resetting the router   ⓑ rebooting her computer

3   Which department does Ray Stevens work in?
ⓐ IT   ⓑ HR

4   What color is the light on the fax machine display?
ⓐ red   ⓑ green

B   Summarize the dialogues.

offline	reconnecting	reboot	language	technician	install

In dialogue 1, Janice is having a problem adjusting the 1_____ settings on her computer. Kenny already solved this problem with his computer last week, so he offers to help. He advises Kelly to 2_____ her computer, but she has already tried that. He tells her to 3_____ the newest version of the operating system. Janice will try that solution next.

In dialogue 2, Ray Stevens from the human resources department calls the IT department, and Sharon answers the phone. Ray tells Sharon that he needs an IT 4_____ because the fax machine is 5_____. Sharon advises Ray to turn the machine off and on again, but it doesn't work. Next, he tries 6_____ the cable, but it also doesn't work. The light on the fax machine is blinking red, so Sharon will send a technician at 11:30.

Don't forget !

We often use the term "down" instead of "broken" when we're talking about technology. For example, "The Internet is down" or "The printer is down."

Read what your colleague has to say and fill in the blanks with your own answers, using the hints on the side.

Practice A

Colleague	Hi, do you need help with something?
You	Hello. 1 _____ ⟵ Explain the problem with your fax machine.
Colleague	Oh, I see. What have you tried so far?
You	I've tried 2 _____ ⟵ Explain the solution that you tried.
Colleague	OK. Did you try reconnecting the cable?
You	Yes, but it still isn't working. 3 _____ ⟵ Request an IT technician.
Colleague	No problem, we'll send someone over. Is there anything else?
You	4 _____ ⟵ Request more printer paper.

Practice B

Colleague	Were you able to solve that internet problem?
You	Yes, it was no big deal. 1 _____ ⟵ Explain how you fixed it.
Colleague	OK, good. We need it for that conference call later.
You	Yes, I'm glad we didn't need to call the IT technician.
Colleague	By the way, I'm heading to the supply closet. Do you need anything?
You	Yes, actually! 2 _____ ⟵ Request a box of staples.
Colleague	Sure, I'll grab a box for you. Anything else?
You	3 _____ ⟵ Explain that the break room needs coffee.
Colleague	All right, I'll ask the office manager about that.
You	Thanks. By the way, 4 _____ ⟵ Explain the problem with the printer.
Colleague	Oh, really? Maybe I can fix it myself. I'll take a look when I get back.
You	Thanks so much!

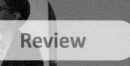

A **Fill in the blanks with the missing words.**

| jammed | cable | reset | convert |

1   You need to _____ the router and set a new WIFI password.

2   I need to print this right away, but our printer is _____ .

3   I'll _____ the file to the right format and send it to you in an email.

4   The _____ is disconnected. I think that's the problem.

B **Choose the correct word(s) or the phrase to complete each sentence.**

1   The fax machine isn't broken. You just need to replace the ink _____ .
   ⓐ cartridge   ⓑ container   ⓒ carton

2   We're out of coffee in the _____ .
   ⓐ supply closet   ⓑ break room   ⓒ rest area

3   You're using an old _____ of the software. You need to update it.
   ⓐ edition   ⓑ version   ⓒ format

C **Choose the expressions from the box to complete the dialogue in order.**

> ⓐ It's not connecting to the internet.
> ⓑ I just need to adjust the sharing permissions so that you can access it.
> ⓒ Let's try resetting the router.

A   Have you sent me that file? We need to submit it by 2:00.

B   Not yet. I'm having a problem with my computer.

A   Yeah? What seems to be the problem?

B   1_____ I haven't been able to access my email since we got back from lunch.

A   I'm having the same problem with my computer. 2_____ Sometimes that works.

B   ... OK, it's working now. I'm having trouble opening that file you sent me.

A   I think I know why. 3_____

B   Sounds good. Just let me know when it's ready.

D Choose the correct words to complete each sentence.

1 You need to (reboot/startup) your computer.

2 The printer is (missing/out of) ink.

3 We need to call the (technician/mechanic).

4 Check the (materials/supply) cabinet for more paper.

E Unscramble the words to make sentences.

1 manager / asked / cartridge / office / I / the / an / ink / for

→ _____

2 printer / paper / in / more / sales / need / we / department / the

→ _____

3 you / resetting / have / ? / router / the / tried

→ _____

4 software / installing / the / is / properly / not

→ _____

F Fill in the blanks with the given words from the box.

IT technician	down	printer paper	supply closet	rebooting

A Hi, there. I'm Hannah Kim. I just started today, in the purchasing department. Are you the office manager?

B Yes, right. My name's Ken Rogers. It's a pleasure to meet you, Hannah.

A You too, Ken. Do you know where I can find the 1_____?

B Sure, the 2_____ is right over there. You can help yourself.

A Oh, thanks. Actually, I'm having a problem with my computer. I wonder if you could help me.

B We have an 3_____ that usually helps with that, but if it's something simple I can try to help.

A I'm not sure what the problem is. My computer is not connecting to the internet.

B Yeah, that happens sometimes. Have you tried 4_____ your computer? That often works for me.

A Yeah, I tried that, but it's still not working. Maybe the WIFI is 5_____?

A Well, it's working for me, so I don't think that's the problem. I think I should ask the IT guy to come and have a look. That's your desk over there?

B Yes, right. Thanks a lot, I really appreciate your help.

03

Managing Schedules and Tasks

Managing schedules and tasks is an important part of office communication. This unit will introduce the essential expressions and vocabulary to delegate tasks and talk about your schedule.

A **Match each question 1–3 with two responses a–f.**

1 Are you free on Friday at 3:00?

2 What should I work on next?

3 What's your role in this project?

a I need you to review the customer feedback.

b You could send out the supplier contracts.

c That works for me.

d Melissa put me in charge of budgeting.

e Actually, my schedule is a little tight.

f I'm overseeing the sales team.

B **When you schedule an appointment, what do you say?**

charge	oversee	need	project	due

It's a large **1**_____, so the whole team will be involved. Jose will **2**_____ the sales team, and Andre will be in **3**_____ of creating a new advertising approach. I **4**_____ you to work with Charles to design packaging. It's **5**_____ next month so we need to get started right away.

Making appointments

These expressions are important for making and managing appointments

What time/day works for you?
- I'm available at 5:00.
- I'm free between 3:00 and 5:00.
- I'm available from 3:00 to 5:00.
- I'm free on Monday.

Does Monday/5:00 work for you?
- Yes, Monday suits me fine.
- Yes, I'll see you then.
- I'm sorry, my schedule is a little tight on Monday.
- No, sorry. Can we make it Tuesday?

I'm sorry, I need to reschedule our meeting.
Can we push back our meeting to 5:30?

Talking about your schedule

These are common expressions when discussing your work schedule.

I'm totally swamped.
I've got too much on my plate.
I've got some time to spare.
My schedule is wide open.
I need to stay late tonight.
I've been doing a lot of overtime lately.
I think I'll get off at 7:00 today.
My boss told me to come in early tomorrow.

Delegating tasks

These expressions will help you assign tasks to your employees or colleagues.

You'll be in charge of the design process.
Mary will oversee the marketing plan.
Andre is responsible for training new employees.
What should I work on next?
- I need you to create a new logo. (strong)
- Maybe you could create a new logo. (weak)
- I would like you to respond to client emails.
- Could you please help Samantha with the marketing plan?
- I think you should order more supplies for the new office.
- Why don't you create some new advertising images?

Talking about deadlines

These expressions are necessary when discussing project deadlines.

When is that project due?
- It's due next Friday.
- We need to turn it in next Friday.
- The deadline is next Friday.
- It should be done by Friday at the latest.

Circle the best response.

1   When is the project due?

   A I am available today.   B I'm free on Monday at 3:00.   C We should turn it in on Monday.

2   Are you off work yet?

   A I need to stay late today.   B The deadline is Tuesday morning.
   C I need to come in early today.

3   Does Friday work for you?

   A Yes, my schedule is a little tight.   B Yes, Friday suits me fine.   C No, Friday is wide open.

4   What time works for you?

   A I did a lot of overtime this week.   B I'm available from 1:00 to 2:00.
   C I've got some time to spare.

5   What time do you start work?

   A I usually stay until 8:00.   B I'm available at 9:00.   C I come in at 7:30.

Real Business English

Using "this" and "next" with days of week(this Friday, next Friday...) can be very confusing, even for native English speakers. If there is any possibility of misunderstanding, there are a few ways to make your intended meaning clearer.

e.g.   (Today is Wednesday, September 13)
   The director is coming **on** Friday. (meaning: September 15)
   The director is coming **this upcoming** Friday. (meaning: September 15)
   The director is coming **next** Friday, the Friday after **this** one. (meaning: September 22)

Listen to the dialogue below and fill in the blanks.

1

A Hi, Chen, how are things?

B Pretty good, Barbara. So, tell me about this new marketing project. Are you **1** _____ the project timeline?

A Yes, I'm the taskmaster, I suppose. I put James Conway **2** _____ the market strategy. Do you know James?

B Yes, we worked together on a project last year. I think he's a good choice for that.

A Yeah, I hope so. And Priya is **3** _____ managing the budget.

B Sounds good to me. Is there anything I can help with?

A Actually, if you've got time, **4** _____ with James and share ideas. I'm sure he would appreciate the help.

B Sure, I'd be happy to help him get started. When is the deadline?

A It needs to be done by October 15th **5** _____ .

2

A Hey Raj, Let's set up a meeting for next week and we'll get started on this project.

B Great. What day works best for you, Alexandre?

A Let me check my schedule… I'm totally **1** _____ on Monday… but my schedule is **2** _____ on Tuesday morning.

B Oh, my schedule is a little **3** _____ in the mornings. Can we make it Wednesday?

A Yes, Wednesday would be fine. What time works for you?

B I have meetings right after lunch until 3:00, but I'm free after that.

A All right. I usually **4** _____ on Wednesdays to pick up my daughter from school, but if we can meet at 3:30, it will be fine for me.

B Are you sure? I'm sure we can finish by 4:00 or 4:30 at the latest.

A Yes, that's no problem. Is there anything you want me to do before then?

B Well, **5** _____ do a little research on the competition? I'll prepare a basic project outline for us to discuss.

A Sounds great. See you then!

A Listen to the dialogues again and answer the following questions.

1 What is James Conway responsible for?
ⓐ the budget   ⓑ the market strategy

2 What does Barbara want Chen to do?
ⓐ to share ideas with James   ⓑ to meet the deadline

3 What day did Raj and Alexandre agree to meet?
ⓐ Tuesday   ⓑ Wednesday

4 What did Raj ask Alexandre to do before the meeting?
ⓐ do research on the competition   ⓑ prepare a basic project outline

B Summarize the dialogues.

responsible	deadline	project outline	mornings	marketing	Wednesday

In dialogue 1, Chen is asking his colleague about a new 1_____ project. He learns that James Conway is in charge of market strategy and Priya is 2_____ for the budget. Chen is asked to meet with James and share ideas. The 3_____ for the project is October 15th.

In dialogue 2, Raj and Alexandre are trying to arrange a meeting for next week. Monday doesn't work for Alexandre, and Tuesday 4_____ are not good for Raj, so they decide on 5_____ afternoon. They agree to meet at 3:30. Before the meeting, Alexandre will do some research and Raj will create a 6_____.

Don't forget !

There are many ways to delegate a task, and each one has a strong or weak tone. If you are speaking to a subordinate, it is OK to use more direct language. For example, "You need to call Mr. Freeman." If not, it is common to phrase your request as a question, and to use conditional language to make the request more polite. For example, "If you have time this afternoon, could you call Mr. Freeman?"

Read what your colleague has to say and fill in the blanks with your own answers, using the hints on the side.

Practice A

Colleague	Are you almost finished with the budget report?
You	Yes, I will have it done by the end of the day.
Colleague	Great. In that case, we should set up a meeting.
You	1 _____ ← Ask which day your colleague can meet.
Colleague	I'm free on Tuesday. Does that work for you?
You	No, sorry. 2 _____ ← Explain that you are busy that day.
Colleague	OK. Is there another day that works better for you?
You	3 _____ ← Explain which day you are free.
Colleague	All right, that works for me, too. Are you free at 3:30?
You	Actually, 4 _____ ← Suggest a later time.
Colleague	Yes, that works for me.
You	OK, perfect. 5 _____ ← Finish the conversation and say goodbye.

Practice B

Colleague	What role would you like me to play in the team?
You	1 _____ ← Tell your colleague about her role. (product design)
Colleague	All right, that sounds good to me. Who's in charge of research?
You	2 _____ ← Explain who will fulfill that role.
Colleague	I see. What about Joyce?
You	3 _____ ← Explain Joyce's role on the team. (budgeting)
Colleague	Great! Is there anything you want me to get started on today?
You	Yes. 4 _____ ← Give your colleague a task. (create a few basic sketches)

Review

A **Fill in the blanks with the missing words.**

plate	due	charge	push

1 Could you tell me when the report is _____?

2 Martin is in _____ of finding a location for the event.

3 I'm afraid I just have too much on my _____ this week.

4 If you don't mind, can we _____ back our meeting to 2:30?

B **Choose the correct word(s) or the phrase to complete each sentence.**

1 I need you to _____ early on Friday to finish the report.

ⓐ come in   ⓑ push back   ⓒ get off

2 My schedule is _____ on Mondays.

ⓐ wide open   ⓑ overtime   ⓒ swamped

3 Does Friday at 2:00 _____ for you?

ⓐ oversee   ⓑ work   ⓒ spare

C **Choose the expressions from the box to complete the dialogue in order.**

ⓐ I've been totally swamped for the last two weeks.
ⓑ What is the deadline?
ⓒ I would like you to update the new tax information into the system.

A   I'm a little concerned that we're behind on the finance reports.

B 1 _____

A   They need to be done by next Monday at the latest.

B   The Monday after this Monday, right?

A   Yes, right. 2 _____

B   Yeah, me too. I have a lot on my plate.

A   I'm worried that we won't be able to finish it in time.

B   Is there something I can do to move things forward?

A   Actually, there is. 3 _____

B   No problem, I'll get started on that right away.

D Choose the correct words to complete each sentence.

1 Jonathan is going to be (overseeing/charging) the recruitment process.

2 I've been doing a lot of (overtime/overseeing) this month.

3 I'm free between 3:00 (to/and) 5:00.

4 Sorry, my schedule is a little (tight/free) on Thursday.

E Unscramble the words to make sentences.

1 like / you / early / to / I'd / tomorrow / in / come

→ _____

2 in / charge / team / marketing / the / be / you'll / of

→ _____

3 could / working / old / documents / on / start / maybe / you / the

→ _____

4 the / Tuesday / next / is / report / progress / due

→ _____

F Fill in the blanks with the given words from the box.

make	latest	available	come in early	deadline

A Jeremy, you look pretty tired today. Is everything OK?

B Yes, I just didn't get much sleep last night. I had to 1_____ this morning to prepare for the product pitch. It went really well!

A That's good to hear. When is the 2_____ ?

B We have three weeks to finish it. We need to get ready and start testing by this Friday at the

3_____ .

A I was hoping to meet with you this week to get your help with this report I'm writing.

B I should be able to make some time. What day works for you?

A I'm 4_____ on Wednesday, if you're free.

A Sure, How about 9:00?

B Can we 5_____ it 10:00? I have a breakfast meeting with a client.

A No problem. I'll confirm with you tomorrow.

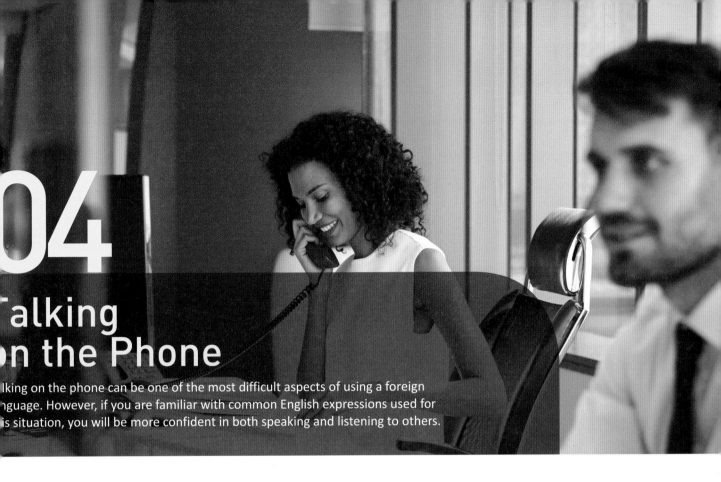

04

Talking on the Phone

Talking on the phone can be one of the most difficult aspects of using a foreign language. However, if you are familiar with common English expressions used for this situation, you will be more confident in both speaking and listening to others.

A Match each question 1–3 with two responses a–f.

1 Hello. May I please speak to Stacy Richards?

2 Hello, Grayson Motors. How can I direct your call?

3 Can I leave a message for her?

a I'm sorry, she's not in at the moment.

b Hi, could you transfer me to the sales department?

c Yes, what would you like me to pass on?

d Just one second. Let me see if she's in.

e Can I speak to Richard Price in HR please?

f Sure, let me grab a pen and notepad.

B When you want to leave a message with a secretary, what do you say?

tell	mobile	regarding	know	reach

Please let her 1_____ that Samuel from the Chicago office called 2_____ her concerns about next month's conference in Singapore. Also, please 3_____ her that I'll be out of the office on Monday and Tuesday, but if she needs to 4_____ me for any reason, she can contact me on my 5_____.

Answering the phone

These expressions can be used to answer the phone professionally in a variety of situations.

Smithson Electronics, how may I help you?
Smithson Electronics, How may I direct your call?
Hello, this is Carlos Sevillano.
Good morning, Carlos Sevillano speaking.
Yes, this is he/she.
Speaking.

Making a call

These expressions will help you sound polite and professional when making a call.

Hello, may I please speak to Carlos Sevillano?
Hi, could you connect/transfer me to the HR department?
Good morning. Carlos Sevillano, please.
Hello, this is Manar Yusef from the Abu Dhabi branch. I'm calling for Carlos Sevillano.

Transferring a call

These expressions are useful for receptionists or secretaries who must direct many calls.

Just one second, let me see if he's in.
Sure, I'll put you through to his office.
Okay, may I ask who's calling?
Could you hold for just a moment?
Could you tell me what it's about?

Taking a message

These expressions are useful for receptionists or secretaries when taking a message.

No, he's not in right now. Can I take a message?
He's taking another call right now. Would you like to hold or leave him a message?
He's out of the office at the moment. Can I take a message?
Would you like to leave a message or would you like him to call you back soon?

Leaving a message

These are some common expressions if you want to leave a message.

Could you just tell him I called?
Please let her know that I called?
She can reach me at 555-6126.
No, that's okay. I'll call her back later.

Checking information

These expressions can be used during those difficult situations in which you can't understand something on the phone.

I'm sorry, could you say that again/repeat that?
I'm sorry, I didn't quite catch that.
Okay, so that's 'M' as in morning, 'A' as in apple, 'N' as is New York, 'A' as apple, and 'R' as in rollercoaster.
Okay, let me read that back to you.

Ending a call

Ending a call can be awkward even for native speakers, but try using these expressions.

Alright, you have a great day. Goodbye now.

Okay, well, call me back tomorrow when you know more.

Okay, I'll talk to you later.

Is there anything else you need help with?

No, that's all. Thank you. Goodbye.

Quiz **Circle the best response.**

1 Hello, can I help you?
   A Let me talk to Janice.   B Hi, could I speak to Janice Ripken, please?
   C I want to talk to Ms. Ripken.

2 Could you transfer me to the IT department?
   A Sure, let me see if he's in.   B Okay, I'll put you through to his office.
   C Could you hold for just a second?

3 Hi, Janice Ripken?
   A Could you tell him I called?   B Speaking.   C She can reach me at 313-9985.

4 He's out of the office at the moment. Can I take a message?
   A It's 614-555-7843   B No, that's okay. Just tell him I called.   C My name is Vihaan Patel.

5 Smithson Electronics, how may I help you?
   A Hi, Carlos Sevillano, please.   B Hello. Who are you?   C Give me Carlos.

🌐 Real Business English

The way we speak in person or with our friends is very different from the polite way we speak on the telephone, especially in business situations. Some expressions that might feel natural are actually very rude or awkward on the phone:

e.g.	Incorrect	Who are you?
	Correct	May I ask who's calling? / To whom am I speaking?
	Incorrect	Are you Marcus Dunham?
	Correct	Is this Marcus Dunham? Am I speaking to Marcus Dunham?
	Incorrect	Hello, I'm Apinya Kittipong. *(in person, it's okay, but not on the phone)*
	Correct	Hello, this is Apinya Kittipong/she.

Listen to the dialogue below and fill in the blanks.

1

A Good morning, Gosling Medical, how may I direct your call?

B Hello, could you 1_____ to Lucia Ballesteros, please?

A Sure, let me see if she's in. May I ask who's calling?

B Yes, this is Jeong-hyun Kim from Fidelity Security.

A Thank you. 2_____ for just a moment?

B Yes, that's fine.

A I'm sorry but it seems that she's out of the office at the moment. Can I 3_____?

B Yes, please. Could you tell her that I'm sorry but I have to cancel lunch tomorrow unfortunately, but I'm available Friday at the same time if she's available.

A I'm sorry, 4_____. Did you say Friday?

B Yes, that's right. Friday at the same time.

A Got it. Can you give me a number where she can reach you?

B Yes, it's 618-2165.

A Okay, I'll pass on your message. 5_____.

B Thank you. Goodbye.

2

A Janix Piping London, Roya Karim here.

B Hi Roya, 1_____ Ji-min at the Seoul branch. I'm calling for Vijay in marketing.

A 2_____?

B I'm calling about some issues related to next month's conference in Chicago.

A Ah, okay. If you could hold for just one moment, I'll transfer you to his office.

B Great. Thanks Roya.

A ... I'm sorry, I'm afraid Vijay is 3_____ at the moment.

B Oh, I see. Do you know when he'll be back?

A I'm not entirely sure, but probably after lunch. 4_____?

B No message, thank you. Could you just tell him I called?

A Sure, not a problem. 5_____?

B No, that's all. Thank you for your help.

A You're welcome. Goodbye now.

B Goodbye.

A Listen to the dialogues again and answer the following questions.

1 What is Jeong-hyun rescheduling?
ⓐ a meeting   ⓑ lunch

2 Where is Lucia Ballesteros right now?
ⓐ not in the office   ⓑ at lunch

3 Ji-min needs information on _____ .
ⓐ the conference   ⓑ the Seoul branch

4 Does Ji-min leave a message?
ⓐ yes   ⓑ no

B Summarize the dialogues.

| cancel | information | Gosling Medical | leaves | office | London |

In dialogue 1, Jeong-hyun is calling 1_____ to talk to Lucia. She wants to 2_____
their lunch appointment for tomorrow and perhaps reschedule for Friday. Lucia isn't in the
office, so Jeong-hyun 3_____ a message for her.

In dialogue 2, Ji-min is looking for 4_____ about the conference in Chicago. She
calls the 5_____ branch of her company and asks to speak to Vijay. He is out of the
6_____ , so Ji-min asks Roya to let Vijay know that she called.

Don't forget !

In Western cultures, it is common to say something friendly and polite at the end of a phone call.
There are many expressions you can use for this, like "You have a nice day," "Have a great day/
weekend," "Have a good one," or "Enjoy the rest of your day."

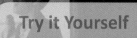

Read what your colleague has to say and fill in the blanks with your own answers, using the hints on the side.

Practice A

Colleague	Hello, my name is Kendrick Rolly.	
You	1 _____	← You don't understand. Politely ask him/her to repeat.
Colleague	Kendrick Rolly. From Rolly Supply.	
You	I'm sorry, 2 _____	← Ask Kendrick to spell his last name.
Colleague	Sure, it's R as in rabbit, O as in octopus, L as in lamp, L as in lamp, Y as in yes.	
You	OK, I got it now, thank you. How can I direct your call?	
Colleague	I'm calling to speak to Mr. Shay in sales.	
You	3 _____	← Politely put him on hold while you transfer him.

Practice B

Colleague	Hello, this is David speaking. How can I help you?	
You	1 _____	← Tell David you are calling for Christian Thomas.
Colleague	OK. Can I have your name, please?	
You	2 _____	← Tell David your name.
Colleague	Sorry, could you spell your first name for me?	
You	3 _____	← Spell your name. Use the technique that Kendrick used in Practice A.
Colleague	Got it. Could you hold for just a moment while I transfer you?	
You	Sure, I'll hold.	
Colleague	I'm sorry, Mr. Thomas is on another call. Would you like to hold or leave a message?	
You	4 _____	← Say that you would like to leave a message.
Colleague	All right, what message would you like me to deliver?	
You	5 _____	← Say that your meeting on Monday has been changed to 10:30 a.m.

A **Fill in the blanks with the missing words.**

speak	call me back	let her know	out of

1 No, that's okay. Just _____ that I called.

2 I'm sorry, but he's _____ the office at the moment.

3 May I please _____ to Ms. Collins in accounting?

4 Okay, well _____ tomorrow if you have a chance.

B **Choose the correct word(s) or the phrase to complete each sentence.**

1 Sure, I'll _____ to her office.

ⓐ transfer   ⓑ call   ⓒ put you through

2 She's taking another _____ right now. Would you like to hold for a moment or leave a message?

ⓐ message   ⓑ call   ⓒ phone

3 She can _____ me at 555-6134.

ⓐ reach   ⓑ leave   ⓒ repeat

C **Choose the expressions from the box to complete the dialogue in order.**

> ⓐ Would you like to hold or leave him a message?
> ⓑ May I ask who's calling?
> ⓒ Could you tell me what it's about?

A Good morning. How can I direct your call?

B Hello. Carlos Villa please.

B 1_____

A This is Jim Cotter calling from Garcia Glassware.

B 2_____

A I'm calling about the status of my order.

B Thank you. Please hold for just a moment.

A Sure, no problem.

B ... I'm sorry, Mr. Villa is taking another call right now. 3_____

A I'll hold, thank you.

B All right, Mr. Villa will be on the line shortly.

D **Choose the correct words to complete each sentence.**

1 (Could/Would) you mind holding?

2 I'm sorry, he's not (in/on/out) at the moment.

3 (Will/May) I please speak to Mr. Gupta?

4 Would you like to (take/leave) a message?

E **Unscramble the words to make sentences.**

1 Kieran / may / speak / please/ to / I / ?

→ _____

2 but / in / I'm / right / she's / now / not / sorry

→ _____

3 him / know / Heather / just / let / called

→ _____

4 may / calling / thanks / Wentz Sportswear / how / ? / for / help / I / you

→ _____

F **Fill in the blanks with the given words from the box.**

moment	transfer	direct	about	let	help

A Good morning, thanks for calling Linux Logistics, how may I 1_____ your call?

B Hi, this is Won-jin Yu from the Shanghai branch. Could you 2_____ me to Jason Rowe?

A I'm sorry, could you spell your last name for me?

B Sure. It's Y as in yellow, U as in umbrella.

A Thank you so much. 3_____ me see if Mr. Rowe is in first... It looks like he's out at the 4_____. Would you like to leave a message?

B No, but please just tell him Won-jin called.

A Okay, is there anything else I can 5_____ you with?

B Actually, could you transfer me to the marketing department?

A Sure, no problem. Could you tell me what this is 6_____?

B I just have a few questions about the advertising plans moving forward.

A All right, thank you. Please hold while I transfer your call.

05

Business Meetings

Participating in a meeting in English can be very intimidating for non-native speakers of English. Practice with these expressions to help you feel more confident, polite, and clear with your communication. You can do it!

A Match each question 1–3 with two proper expressions a–f.

1 How do you open a meeting?

2 How do you ask for opinions?

3 How do you introduce the purpose of the meeting?

a What do you think about this proposal?

b I'd like to thank everyone for coming today.

c We are here to go over our sales.

d If we are all here, let's get started.

e I've called this meeting to make a few announcements.

f How do you feel about this?

B When you want to begin a meeting, what do you say?

opinions	introduced	organized	discuss	meeting

Okay, everyone. Let's get started. I've called this **1**_____ because we need to **2**_____ some problems. I know many of you have strong **3**_____ on these ongoing issues, but I want this meeting to be **4**_____, so please wait for each issue to be **5**_____ before you express your opinion on it.

Opening a meeting

If you are the meeting chair, or leader, you can use these expressions to help you get started.

Okay, can we start please?
If I can have your attention, we're going to start.
Alright, let's begin. / OK, everyone, let's get started.
I've called this meeting to discuss next month's conference.
The purpose/reason/aim for this meeting is to go over our sales.
We're here today to discuss the marketing concept for our new product.

Asking for and giving opinions and suggestions

These expressions are perhaps the most useful for having a successful and productive meeting.

What do you think about hiring more marketers?
- In my opinion, the HR department is making a big mistake.

What's your opinion on this?
- I think we should stay with the same strategy.
- Actually, I don't like the idea of changing our supplier.
- I'm (not) in favor of increasing investment in R&D.

What are your thoughts on our supplier problems?
How do you feel about this?
- Maybe we should sell some equipment.
- Well, we could advertise more on public transportation.

Agreeing and Disagreeing

Agreeing is the easy part. With disagreeing, however, you must be gentler.

Okay, I see your point.
Yes, I suppose you're right.
I (completely/totally/strongly) agree.
I couldn't agree more.
I'm not so sure that they will work.
I'm not sure if I agree.
I'd have to disagree on that.
I'm afraid I disagree.
I (completely/totally/strongly) disagree.

Managing and closing the meeting

These expressions are great for someone who is chairing the meeting and must keep the discussion orderly.

Do you have a question?
Okay, do we all agree on this?
Now, I think we should discuss our image problems.
Let's move on to the next item on our agenda.

Okay, let's recap/go over our conclusions.
Does anyone have anything else to add?
If there's nothing else, let's get back to work.
Email me if you have any further questions or concerns.

Interrupting and handling interruptions

It's okay to politely interrupt sometimes, but you should know these expressions to interrupt and handle interruptions properly.

Sorry, but could I say something real quick?

I'm sorry to interrupt, but can I say something real quick?

Can I just add something to that?

I'd like to say something.

Sure, go ahead. (accepting interruptions)

Can we come back to that point later?

Just give me one more second to finish.

I'm sorry, but we need to move on.

Quiz

Circle the best response.

1 Do you agree or disagree?

   A I want to talk now.   B I couldn't agree more.   C Let's get back to work.

2 What are your thoughts on the new marketing strategies?

   A Let's go over our conclusions.   B Can I add something to that?

   C I'm not so sure that they will work.

3 Does anyone else have something to add?

   A Yes, I'd like to say something.   B Let's get started.   C I completely agree.

4 Could I just add something to that?

   A Let's recap what we have covered.   B They are making a big mistake.   C Sure, go ahead.

5 Do we all agree on this?

   A Please continue.   B I totally agree.   C Let's go over our conclusion.

 Real Business English

Remember, "be quiet" is very strong, and "shut up" is even stronger. We usually only use these expressions if we are very annoyed or angry. If you want to politely ask someone to stop speaking, try these more indirect and polite expressions:

e.g. If you could, please keep it down. ("to keep it down" means to not be loud)

Okay, let's quiet down so that we can get started. (good for a group)

Could I have your attention, please? (if someone is being rude and talking while someone else is talking)

Listen to the dialogue below and fill in the blanks.

1

A Good morning, everyone. If I could have **1**_____, we're going to start. I've **2**_____ this meeting to discuss strategies to increase sales in our southeast market. The first item on the agenda is clarifying why sales have decreased so much. The CEO is getting really frustrated and we need to take action now. Min-jeong, What's your **3**_____ on this?

B **4**_____, sales have decreased because we simply aren't doing enough market research to find out what the consumer wants. I'm in favor of an aggressive new marketing campaign in every major city in the Southeast. I'm sure the CEO would agree. **5**_____?

A **6**_____. I also recently heard our top competitors in the area are outselling us because they have the latest market research. Maybe we need to do the same.

2

A Okay, let's move on to the next...

B Amanda, wait, can I just **1**_____ to that before we move on? I think it's really important.

A Sure, **2**_____ James.

B Well, I'm not so sure that we should place such a big order just before the holidays. **3**_____ for the last few holiday seasons, sales have slumped. Typically, we don't get busy again until late January. We could save some money now if we put in a smaller order.

A **4**_____, but honestly, I'm **5**_____ with you. Our advertising agency is marketing our product line right now as a Christmas gift idea. I think we could see a huge jump in sales, so we should be ready. Also, if sales aren't very high, it's okay if we have a little extra in stock. We have the space in the warehouse, so it won't be a big problem.

A Listen to the dialogues again and answer the following questions.

1 What is the reason for meeting 1?
   ⓐ to discuss the already decreasing sales in the southeast market.
   ⓑ to discuss the recently increased sales in the southeast market

2 What are Min-jeong's thoughts on the problem?
   ⓐ that they need more market research   ⓑ that the market research is low quality

3 James has concerns about the _____ .
   ⓐ Christmas   ⓑ the size of the order

4 At first, the meeting chair, Amanda wanted to _____ .
   ⓐ finish the meeting   ⓑ discuss the next item on the agenda

B Summarize the dialogues.

interrupted	purpose	opinion	move on	attention	opens	sales	concern

In dialogue 1, the chair 1 _____ the meeting and asks everyone politely for their
2 _____ . The chair then states the 3 _____ of the meeting, which is the poor
4 _____ in their southeast market. He then asks Min-jeong, for her 5 _____ , and
she says they need to do more research. He agrees with her.

In dialogue 2, the chair tries to 6 _____ to the next point, but he is 7 _____ by
James who wishes to add an opinion. James then expresses his 8 _____ over the big
order before the holidays. The chair politely interrupts, expresses her disagreement with
James's idea, and gives her reasons.

Don't forget !

Remember, in many Western, English-speaking cultures, meeting participants are encouraged
equally to contribute and express their opinion openly, regardless of their position in the
company's hierarchy. If you are a lower-level employee at a meeting, it's okay to express your
opinion or even politely interrupt to do so.

Read what your colleague has to say and fill in the blanks with your own answers, using the hints on the side.

Practice A

Colleague   Okay, let's quiet down so that we can move on to the next item. Now, I'd like to propose finishing our project earlier than scheduled. How do you feel about this?

You   Well, 1_____ We've had problems meeting deadlines in the past.
— Politely say that you don't like the idea.

Colleague   Yes, I suppose you're right. I think the 15th would be a reasonable deadline.

You   2_____ Maybe we should push it to the 20th.
— Gently disagree.

Colleague   Okay, that's fine. Well, I think we've covered everything, so...

You   3_____ We still need to go over the sales figures for last quarter.
— Interrupt politely.

Colleague   I know that was on the agenda, but we have not received the report from the accounting department yet.

You   Okay, I understand. 4_____ — Ask when the report will be ready.

Colleague   They told me it would be finished by noon today.

You   Got it. I'll stop by their office after lunch and pick it up.

Practice B

Colleague   I think we've covered everything.

You   1_____ — You are the chair. End the meeting.

Colleague   Just one more thing, I think it might be better to tell PR first. Plus,...

You   2_____ We don't have the time to talk about PR issues right now.
— Reject this interruption.

Colleague   I understand, we can discuss it later.

You   But before we go, I just want to ask your opinion on the upcoming conference.

3_____ — Ask your colleague for their opinion.

Colleague   I think the plan looks excellent, but we need to make sure it will fit within our budget.

You   4_____ We will ask the project manager for a detailed expense estimate.
— Agree with your colleague.

A Fill in the blanks with the missing words.

feel	thoughts	opinion	think

1 What's your _____ on the new construction plan?

2 How do you _____ about transferring to our Honolulu office??

3 What do you _____ about our new slogan?

4 What are your _____ on the new product designs?

B Choose the correct word(s) or the phrase to complete each sentence.

1 Okay, let's _____ what we've discussed.
   ⓐ talk   ⓑ go over   ⓒ think

2 Let me _____ my point.
   ⓐ finish   ⓑ stand   ⓒ tell

3 Hmmm, I'm not so _____ .
   ⓐ agree   ⓑ opinion   ⓒ sure

C Choose the expressions from the box to complete the dialogue in order.

ⓐ what's your opinion on this?
ⓑ let's get started.
ⓒ can I have your attention, please?

A Good morning, everyone. 1 _____ I'm excited for today's meeting. It looks like we've got some great news to discuss. William, 2 _____

B Oh, I'm sorry. I was just telling Jacques about the great numbers we're getting from our branch in Malaysia. It looks like they sent the figures last night. It seems like Malaysia could be our next big market!

A Yes, that's the reason why I've called this meeting. Marsha, 3 _____ Do you think we can maintain this kind of success in Malaysia? I'm worried that customers are just interested in our products because they're new.

D Choose the correct words to complete each sentence.

1 I strongly (agree / in favor). I think it's a great idea.

2 Okay, I think that's about everything. Does anyone have anything else to (complain about / add)?

3 Just give me one (second / word) to finish.

4 Okay, I see your (saying / point).

E Unscramble the words to make sentences.

1 conclusions / over / go / our / let's

   → _____

2 discuss / new HR problems / the / is / the purpose / of / to / this meeting

   → _____

3 the legal / what / issues / are / your thoughts / on / ?

   → _____

4 email / if / questions or concerns / have / me / you / any further

   → _____

F Fill in the blanks with the given words from the box.

agenda	started	brainstorm	opinions	called	ideas

Hello everyone, may I have your attention, please? Let's get 1_____.
I've 2_____ this meeting today to discuss the upcoming sales event we're
having in Denver, and I was hoping to get all of your 3_____. We really need
to work together on this since the board members are not pleased. Our last two sales events were
dismal, so we need to
4_____ together to find ways it can go more smoothly this time. I know that
many of you have mentioned some great ideas. However, I think we should all agree on two or
three to get started. The first item on the 5_____ is the lackluster display tents.
I think we should get tents that really get a lot of attention. John, what's your 6_____ on
this?

48

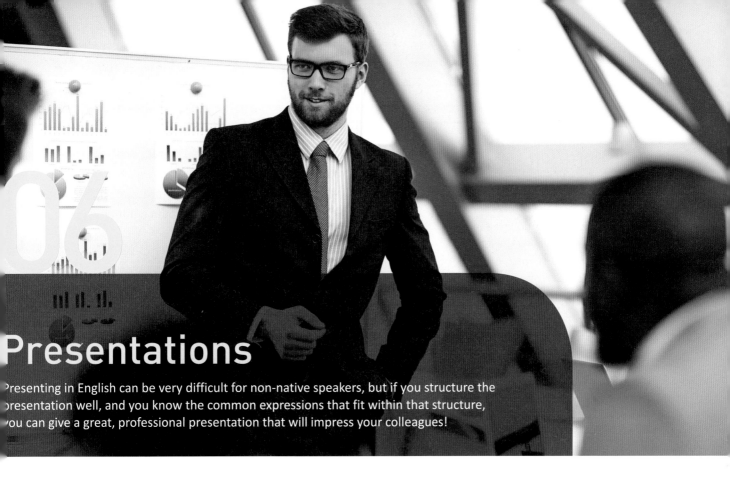

Presentations

Presenting in English can be very difficult for non-native speakers, but if you structure the presentation well, and you know the common expressions that fit within that structure, you can give a great, professional presentation that will impress your colleagues!

Warm up

A **Match each question 1–3 with two proper expressions a–f.**

1 What is the best way to introduce yourself in a presentation?

2 What's the best way to transition to a new section of a presentation?

3 What's the best way to conclude a presentation?

a Okay, now let's move on to the stats.

b And that concludes my presentation.

c Hi, everyone. I'm Jake from the PR department. Thanks for coming.

d Thank you so much for listening. Does anyone have any questions?

e Good morning everyone, I'm the Head of Marketing for On Point Logistics.

f Let's take a look at the next part of my presentation

B **When you want to introduce your presentation, what do you say?**

lastly	after that	divided	first	like

Today, I'd **1**_____ to talk about some important aspects of sales in the publishing industry. I've **2**_____ my presentation into three parts. **3**_____, I'll go over the basics of successful sales in the industry. **4**_____, we'll look at how sales in publishing is changing rapidly. And **5**_____, I'll discuss the future of the industry.

Presentation introductions

There are several key aspects to a presentation introduction: self-intro, purpose, outline, stating the length, instruction for questions.

My name is Rosa Dominguez and I'm a Product Designer for Franklin Furniture.

I'm here today to discuss my company's greatest goals.

The purpose of my presentation is to introduce our new sales strategies.

I've divided my presentation into three parts.
- First, I'll discuss my company's newest innovations.
- Secondly/Next/After that, we'll look at new features.
- Lastly/Finally, I'll talk about the future of our company.

My presentation will be about ten minutes.

I only need about 10 minutes of your time.

Please feel free to stop me at any time if you have any questions.

You can ask any questions during my presentation.

Please hold any questions for the end of the presentation.

I'll take any questions at the end.

The body of the presentation: transition expressions

It's important to make it clear to the audience that you're moving on to a new section of the presentation to reduce confusion.

First, let's take a look at last year's figures.

Now, we'll move on to our goals for the coming expo.

Okay, moving on to the next section of my presentation.

I'll continue by talking about the added storage space.

Now, I'd like to draw your attention to some new features.

Turning now to our ten-year outlook.

Finally, that brings us to the marketing research.

The body of the presentation: other useful expressions

During the body of your presentation, you can keep your audience's attention with these useful phrases.

If you'll look here, you can see how our sales dropped.

In this slide, you can see the new construction plans.

Now, take a close look at this part of the graph.

You can see here the rise in sales before Christmas.

I must stress the importance of brand image.

I just want to emphasize that we need to increase advertising.

I'd like to highlight that we will be updating all of our software.

Before I move on, does anyone have any questions or comments?

Presentation conclusions

Like the introduction, the conclusion of a presentation needs to be well-structured to sound professional.

And that brings me to the end of my presentation.

And that concludes my presentation.

And I believe that's about everything for my presentation.

To sum up, we've gone over last month's sales figures, latest innovations, and global customer service.

To recap, the three main points of this presentation are that we're downsizing our legal department, hiring more PR reps, and considering moving to a new office next year.
To conclude, don't forget that we have excellent discounts for repeat customers.
You've been a great audience.
Thank you so much for your attention.
I'd be happy to take a few questions now.

Quiz

Circle the best response.

1 You want to introduce yourself at a formal conference.
   A Now, let's move on.   B Thank you so much for listening to my presentation.
   C Good morning everyone, I'm Rick and I'm a new product designer at Amped Stereo.

2 You want to start your presentation conclusion.
   A Good morning everyone.   B And that brings me to the end of my presentation.
   C I'm Rick from Amped Stereo.

3 You want to draw attention to a graph in one of your slides.
   A Now, take a close look at this graph here.   B To conclude, we have the best sales figures.
   C Thank you all for coming.

4 You want to transition from one section of your presentation to another.
   A Welcome to my presentation.   B Take a close look at this slide.
   C Okay, moving on to the next section of my presentation.

Real Business English

Remember, it's sometimes possible to give a much more informal presentation in the business world, especially when you're talking to close colleagues. A good tip to remember is:
formal = longer expressions, informal = shorter expressions

e.g.   Formal   Now, if I could draw your attention to the graph on the left, you'll see how our sales have increased dramatically in the last two years.

Informal   Take a look at the slide on the left. You can see how sales have jumped in the last two years.

Listen to the presentation and fill in the blanks.

1

Good afternoon, everyone. **1**_____ Rick Stevenson, the lead product designer for Amped Stereo. The **2**_____ of my presentation is to familiarize you all with our latest innovations so that you can get a better idea if our systems are right for your businesses. I've **3**_____ my presentation into three parts. First, I'll discuss the improvements on our existing products. **4**_____, we'll look at some of our exciting new products. Finally, I'll talk about why our innovations can help your businesses. **5**_____ about ten minutes of your time, and please don't be afraid to interrupt me if you have any questions.

2

Now, **1**_____ to our exciting new products. **2**_____ at this picture above, you'll see our most powerful speaker yet. **3**_____. How many of you here are tired of moving around several huge speakers for your big events? Well, now you'll only need one: the Amped SR2000 MegaSound Speaker. I'd just **4**_____ that for the price, this speaker will give you triple the sound of your current speakers.

3

And that **1**_____ my presentation. **2**_____, we've gone over the latest improvements on our products that you already know and love, our exciting new line of products, and why we're the best for your business. **3**_____, I hope you keep in mind that we have the top-selling audio and stereo products in the country for the last 4 years for a reason, as I've shown you today. **4**_____ for coming. Now, **5**_____, feel free to ask.

A Listen to the presentation again and answer the following questions.

1 What is the main topic of Rick's presentation?
   ⓐ Amped Stereo's great sales   ⓑ Amped Stereo's innovations

2 What should the audience do if they have any questions?
   ⓐ interrupt Rick   ⓑ wait until the end of the presentation

3 What is Rick's promise regarding the new SR2000 MegaSound Speaker?
   ⓐ that the audience should buy three   ⓑ that it's as powerful as three speakers.

4 What kind of presentation do you think this is?
   ⓐ B2B sales presentation   ⓑ meeting presentation for coworkers

B Summarize the presentation intro and conclusion.

remark   questions   instructs   greets   summarizes   innovations   thanks   outlines

In the presentation intro, Rick **1**_____ his audience and introduces himself.
He's presenting his company's **2**_____ to business owners. He **3**_____ his
presentation by telling the audience how he's divided the presentation. He **4**_____ the
audience to interrupt him if he has any questions.

In the presentation body, Rick talks about the amazing new SR2000 MegaSound Speaker and
talks about how powerful it is. In the conclusion, Rick **5**_____ his three main points.
Then, he gives a strong concluding **6**_____ for the audience to remember. Finally, he
7_____ the audience and asks them if they have any **8**_____ .

Don't forget !

Remember, the presentation structure that you've studied so far is a bit flexible. It may be possible to change the order of some of these elements, and it may be possible to add extra elements to create an entertaining style. For example, you could include a quick story or an amazing fact to your presentation introduction to grab the attention of the audience.

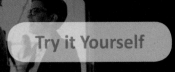

Complete the presentation introduction, body and conclusion excerpt with your own answers, using the hints on the side.

Practice A

— Greet your audience formally.

1 _____ My name is David Kim and I'm s Senior Sales Rep. for

Techno Electronics. 2 _____ to tell you all about our wonderful
— Tell the purpose.

products. 3 _____ First, I'll discuss our products' durability and
— Introduce your outline.

longevity. After that, we'll look at our products' unique features. Finally, we'll go over the

great deals we're offering on our latest products. 4 _____ Please

hold any questions for the end of the presentation.
— Tell your audience the length of your presentation.

Practice B

— Use a transition expression to show that this is the last section of the presentation and it is about deals.

1 _____ We offer fantastic

deals on PCs for your office no matter what your needs. 2 _____,
— Refer to the chart.

we offer almost 30% discounts for orders of 500 or more units. Also, 3 _____
— Emphasize this point.

all of the installation is free and done by our expert tech guys. 4 _____
— Start the conclusion.

To recap, our products are the most durable, have the newest features, and will save you

money. In conclusion, I hope you keep in mind how much Techno products can help your

company in the future. Thank you so much for your attention. Now, if you have any questions,

feel free to ask.

Review

A **Fill in the blanks with the missing words.**

concludes	for coming	emphasize	attention

1 Hello and thank you _____.

2 I just want to _____ that this decrease in sales will be temporary.

3 And that _____ my presentation.

4 Thank you so much for your _____.

B **Choose the correct word(s) or the phrase to complete each sentence.**

1 _____, we've gone over our marketing research, our plans for the coming months, and our possible expansion plans for next year.

ⓐ To discuss ⓑ To summary ⓒ To sum up

2 _____, you can see how we've been doing well in our North African region.

ⓐ If you'll look here ⓑ Look at that ⓒ I show you here

3 You've been a great _____.

ⓐ people ⓑ crowded ⓒ audience

C **Choose the expressions from the box to complete the presentation in order.**

ⓐ You can see here
ⓑ First, let's take a look
ⓒ I'd like to highlight

1 _____ at our latest innovations. We're confident that our company has the most advanced technology of any security company. We've moved on from pin pads and electronic keys to futuristic eye and fingerprint scanners. 2 _____ in the video, we have the most secure fingerprint technology to ensure the security of your buildings.

3 _____ that this technology is very easy to set up and use. We can have your entire building secured in just a few days. You'll have the peace of mind to know that intruders aren't breaking in and stealing information.

D Choose the correct words to complete each sentence.

1 In this slide, you can (view / see) our biggest warehouse, which is in Detroit.

2 First, I'll (chat / talk) about our company's history.

3 Please feel (good / free) to interrupt me if you have any questions.

4 I must (stress / feel) the importance of the reduced overall cost to your company.

E Unscramble the words to make sentences.

1 welcome / thank / everyone / coming / for / and / you

→ _____

2 happy / a few / take / questions / I'd be / now / to

→ _____

3 presentation / three / divided / my / into / parts / I've

→ _____

4 today / I'm / to discuss / my company's / here / products / latest

→ _____

F Fill in the blanks with the given words from the box.

| you've been | questions | everything | to recap | to conclude |

And I believe that's about 1_____ for my presentation. 2_____,
the three main points of my presentation are our company's impeccable reliability, renowned
customer service, and excellent bulk discounts. 3_____, I hope you will consider
us for all of your printing needs, as I can guarantee that we will not only save your company money,
but you will streamline the ordering process in order to save time as well.

4_____ a great audience and thanks for coming. Now, if you have any 5_____,
please feel free to ask. Also, don't forget to take one of my cards on the way out.

07

Product Marketing

Selling a product or service is the core of most successful businesses. This unit will give you the necessary vocabulary and expressions to market and advertise what your company has to offer.

A **Match each question 1–3 with two responses a–f.**

1   What are the best features of this product?

2   What are we doing to improve our marketing efforts?

3   What kind of promotions are we offering?

a   It comes in a variety of styles.

b   We recently hired an SEO specialist to improve our social media marketing.

c   We're offering a 10% discount next month.

d   We are rebranding the product for a new market.

e   For gold members, we're providing free overnight delivery.

f   It's a very user-friendly design.

B **When you describe a product, what do you say?**

practical	colors	durable	in	of

These jeans come 1_____ three different styles, and they are made 2_____ high-quality materials. They are very 3_____, so they last a long time. And the design is 4_____, so they are perfect for everyday use. We offer them in two 5_____ – blue and black.

Describing products

Use these expressions to describe the products you are selling.

It's made of high-quality materials.
It's a best-selling product in its category.
These shoes are remarkably durable.
It's very practical for everyday use.
It's extremely versatile with various uses.
The interface is extremely user-friendly.
It comes in a variety of colors.
It's made of leather/wood/plastic.
They sell for $500.

Marketing a product

These expressions will help you discuss marketing strategies with your team.

What is our target market?
- We are targeting young business professionals.

We're conducting market research this month.
The target market is teenage boys.
The sales forecast is quite promising.
We haven't received the sales figures for last month.
We're launching an advertising campaign in April.
Our advertising budget is smaller than I expected.
We are hiring an outside ad agency.
We really need to rebrand this product for a new market.
The market for tablets is pretty saturated at the moment.

Digital marketing

These expressions are useful for talking about digital marketing strategies.

This banner ad is generating a lot of leads.
We need more engagement on our social media pages.
Our SEO specialist is getting us a lot of hits.
The conversion rate for this video ad is too low.
We should consider hiring an influencer to review the product.
It looks like our jeans are trending on social media.

Advertising and Promotion

Use these expressions in your product advertising and promotions.

The summer sale ends on August 15th.
Buy two for the price of one!
We're offering a 25% discount this week.
This model is available for a limited time only.
We offer a money-back guarantee for 30 days.
Free delivery anywhere within the country.
Get exclusive discounts with a gold membership.

Circle the best response.

1 Tell me about the winter sale.

   A It comes in a variety of colors.   B These shoes are trending on social media.
   C It ends at the end of the month.

2 What is this jacket made of?

   A Leather.   B Red.   C Three styles.

3 Is this bag versatile?

   A Yes, you can use it in many situations.   B Yes, it's perfect for a formal event.
   C Yes, the style is very practical.

4 Has the banner ad been effective?

   A Yes, it is very user-friendly.   B Yes, we have asked an influencer to promote it.
   C Yes, it has generated a lot of leads.

5 What are the benefits of the Platinum Membership?

   A The sales forecast looks excellent.   B You get exclusive discounts on every item.
   C It's made of very durable materials.

Real Business English

When describing a product, you might find yourself using the word "very" a lot. The car is "very fast," "very stylish," or "very reliable." To add more variety to your description, try using different words instead of "very." Here are some ideas:

extremely	amazingly	surprisingly
incredibly	remarkably	uniquely
unbelievably	exceptionally	strikingly

Listen to the dialogue below and fill in the blanks.

1

A   Lucas, how's it going?

B   Hi Alice, I'm doing well. We just got the **1**_____ on that new bicycle helmet we released a few months ago, and they're better than we anticipated.

A   Oh that's good! Which helmet are you talking about? The red and green one?

B   Actually, it comes in **2**_____ and patterns. But the black and white model has been our best seller.

A   Oh, I see. So how is this new helmet different from the standard model?

B   Well, it's more **3**_____, for a start. It's practically indestructible. It's made from extremely high-quality materials.

A   I'm glad it's selling so well. The marketing team must be doing a good job.

B   Yes, even with a relatively small **4**_____ they've done quite well.

A   How did they do it?

B   They launched a really impressive social media **5**_____. We've managed to get a few influencers to do video reviews, and that helped a lot.

A   Sounds great. I should suggest that to my team as well.

B   Yes, I totally recommend it.

2

A   Excuse me, would you like some help?

B   Actually, I'm just browsing.

A   OK, well let me know if you have any questions.

B   Actually, I was looking at this dress. Does it **1**_____ any other sizes?

A   Yes, that's the 5 there, but we also have it in a 4 and a 6.

B   OK, I think I'll try on the 4 if that's all right.

A   Of course, no problem. I love that dress, actually. My wife has one at home. It's so **2**_____, you can wear it anywhere.

B   Is it 100% cotton?

A   Actually, it's **3**_____ an 80% cotton blended fabric. It actually helps to prevent wrinkles, and it breathes really well.

B   Oh, looking at the price, I'm afraid it's a little expensive for me.

A   Well, we're offering a **4**_____ on all dresses until the end of the week. You should also consider joining our membership program for an extra 5% discount.

B   Do I need to pay anything to join?

A   No, it's totally free. You'll get **5**_____ discounts on our online store as well.

B   All right, well, thanks for the information. Where can I find the fitting room?

A Listen to the dialogues again and answer the following questions.

1 What is the most popular helmet model?
ⓐ red and green   ⓑ black and white

2 Why was the marketing team successful?
ⓐ they used social media   ⓑ they had a large advertising budget

3 How many sizes does the dress come in?
ⓐ two   ⓑ three

4 What is the total discount the customer can get on the dress?
ⓐ 20%   ⓑ 15%

B Summarize the dialogues.

comes in	bicycle helmet	5% discount	social media	variety	price

In dialogue 1, Lucas tells Alice about the success of their new 1_____. It comes in a 2_____ of colors and patterns, and it is very durable. The marketing team had a small budget, but their 3_____ campaign was very successful.

In dialogue 2, a customer asks a store attendant about a dress. The dress 4_____ three sizes, and it is made of an 80% cotton blend. The 5_____ is a little high, but there is a 15% discount on all dresses in the store. The customer can get an additional 6_____ by joining their membership program.

Don't forget !

Many customers from western countries prefer to browse the store without the help of a staff member. Instead of following a customer around the store, it is recommended to let the customer know you are willing to help, and then let them browse on their own. You can say, "Are you looking for anything in particular?" or "I'll be right over here if you need any help with anything."

Read what your colleague has to say and fill in the blanks with your own answers, using the hints on the side.

Practice A

| Colleague | How is the marketing campaign for the new car going? |
| You | It's going well. 1_____ ← Tell your colleague about the sales forecast. |

| Colleague | How about the digital marketing? |
| You | 2_____ ← Explain the success you are having on social media. |

| Colleague | That's great news. What do you think is the cause? |
| You | Well, our SEO specialist is doing really good work. |

| Colleague | So what is our target market? |
| You | 3_____ ← Explain your target market. |

| Colleague | Great. What is the main feature we are promoting? |
| You | 4_____ ← Explain the main feature. (user–friendly) |

| Colleague | Excellent. Are you having any difficulties? |
| You | Actually, 5_____ ← Explain the problem. (small advertising budget) |

Practice B

| Colleague | Are you the new social media marketer? |
| You | Yes, right. 1_____ ← Introduce yourself. |

| Colleague | Nice to meet you. I'm Chad Stevens. So what are you working on? |
| You | 2_____ ← Tell Chad what you are doing. (designing a banner ad) |

| Colleague | I see. Have you noticed any problem with our marketing efforts? |
| You | 3_____ ← Explain the low conversion rates for video ads. |

| Colleague | Oh, I didn't realize that. Well, let me know if you need anything. |
| You | 4_____ ← Thank Chad and say goodbye. |

A Fill in the blanks with the missing words.

trending	guarantee	target	sales figures

1 We are offering a 60-day money-back _____.

2 Our new tablet is _____ on social media.

3 Did you see the _____ for last year?

4 I'd like this campaign to _____ older women.

B Choose the correct word(s) or the phrase to complete each sentence.

1 These shoes _____ three different styles.

　　ⓐ try on　　　　　ⓑ come in　　　　　ⓒ are made of

2 The most expensive model _____ $800.

　　ⓐ sells for　　　　　ⓑ comes in　　　　　ⓒ targets

3 We need to hire an outside ad _____.

　　ⓐ research　　　　　ⓑ agency　　　　　ⓒ budget

C Choose the expressions from the box to complete the dialogue in order.

> ⓐ That should create a lot of engagement on our social media pages.
> ⓑ Are we launching a social media campaign as well?
> ⓒ We're going to offer a 30% discount on all of our winter clothing.

A Tell me about the promotion we're launching next month.

B 1 _____

A That's great, that worked really well last year, if I remember right.

B Yes, you're right. We're also going to offer free delivery for online orders.

A Does that apply to international deliveries as well?

B No, the free delivery is just for domestic orders.

A Excellent. 2 _____

B Yes, we're making a series of banner ads offering two for the price of one on our online store.

A That's good. 3 _____

B Yes, I'm hoping for even better results than last year.

D **Choose the correct words to complete each sentence.**

1 We need to conduct more market (research/forecast).

2 We should (rebrand/target) rich people.

3 The pop-up ad is (influencing/generating) a lot of leads.

4 We have a two-for-the-(price/cost)-of-one deal.

E **Unscramble the words to make sentences.**

1 our / user-friendly / phone / is / new / incredibly

→ _____

2 is / item / sweater / our / this / best-selling

→ _____

3 by / last / figures / I / disappointed / am / month's / sales

→ _____

4 need / bigger / budget / a / we / advertising

→ _____

F **Fill in the blanks with the given words from the box.**

| guarantee | durable | made of | ended | versatile |

A Are these shoes available in black?

B No, I'm sorry, we only offer that pair in brown.

A What are they 1_____?

B They're actually 100% leather, with a rubber heel. They are amazingly 2_____.

A Do you think they would be appropriate for a formal event?

B Yes, they're extremely 3_____. You could wear them for almost any occasion.

A All right. I noticed the sign out front. Are these shoes part of the sale?

B Yes, we can offer you a 25% discount on these shoes.

A Oh, that's great. I was worried that the sale was over.

A You're lucky – it 4_____ yesterday, but we extended it one additional day.

B That's great. I'm still a little concerned about spending so much money on one pair of shoes.

A I understand. If you have any problem with them, we offer a two-week money-back 5_____.
But I'm sure you'll really like them.

08

Ordering and Supplying Goods and Services

over the phone, by email, or in person, placing and responding to orders is an important part of business operations. This unit will teach you the expressions and vocabulary necessary to order goods and services naturally.

Warm up

A Match each question 1–3 with two responses a–f.

1 How much is it per unit?

2 Has our order been shipped yet?

3 Could you send us 50 pairs of the black sunglasses?

a It seems that we have not received your payment yet.

b You can see the price list on our website.

c I'm sorry, that item is no longer in stock.

d I'll send an order form for you to fill out.

e The price varies depending on the size of the order.

f The delivery date is December 5th.

B When you place an order, what do you say?

discount	place	offer	price	delivery

Hello, I would like to 1_____ an order for 250 boxes of drinking straws. The 2_____ date is very important, as we need them within 15 days. I saw the 3_____ list on your website, but I was wondering if you 4_____ a 5_____ for ordering in bulk. Thank you for your prompt attention.

Making Enquiries

Use these expressions when asking questions to a supplier.

Hello, can I help you?
- We would like to know more about the types of windows you produce.
- We are interested in purchasing 300 units of cedar plywood.
- I'm calling in reference to our order number 20034.
- I have a question about an order we placed three weeks ago.
- Can I have an update on my order number 945?
- Our order number 33253 has not been delivered.

Do you have any other questions?
- How many solar panels do you have in stock?
- What is your order minimum?
- Do you ship internationally?
- Could we have a price estimate?
- Could you send us a sample of each of those items?

Do you have a question about your order?
- When can we expect to receive the shipment?
- Could you please let me know the delivery date?

Making offers

These are expressions used by suppliers when responding to client enquiries.

What kind of price can you offer?
- You can find our catalog and price list on our website.
- The wholesale price is listed in our catalog.
- If you are planning to buy in bulk, we can offer you a substantial discount.
- We are pleased to make the following offer.

I'll send you an order form for you to fill out.
We look forward to receiving your order.

Placing orders

Use these expressions when you are ready to place an order with a supplier.

I'd like to place an order for 250 units.
We would like to place a purchase order.
We're going to need a two-year contract.
Could you send 100 units as soon as possible?
Could we also have 40 standard patio chairs?

Acknowledging orders

These expressions are used when confirming or following up on an order.

I am pleased to acknowledge receipt of your order number 402.
We are currently processing your order.
We'll confirm by email when your order has been processed.
Your order will be shipped out as soon as we receive your payment.
We have sent you an invoice with instructions for payment.

Circle the best response.

1 How long of a contract are you looking for?

   A I am pleased to acknowledge a 5-year contract.   C We confirm a 5-year contract.

   B We're going to need a 5-year contract.

2 Can I have an update on my order number 6399?

   A We are currently processing your order.   B I'd like to place a purchase order.

   C When can we expect the shipment?

3 Hello, can I help you?

   A We'll confirm your order by email.   B The wholesale price is listed in our catalog.

   C I'm calling in reference to order number 514.

4 What kind of price can you offer?

   A We can offer you a discount for buying in bulk.   B We'll send you an order form to fill out.

   C Your price estimate will be shipped out next week.

5 Do you have any other questions?

   A Could you make the following offer?   B Will I send you an invoice?

   C How many tables do you have in stock?

Real Business English

Business English can be very indirect in comparison to other languages and cultures. We rarely say something like "I want" or "Give me." Instead, we tend to use a lot of indirect questions and other polite language forms to explain what we want.

e.g.   Direct   I want 50 laptops.   Indirect   Could you give me 50 laptops?

Could we order 50 laptops?

Would it be possible to order 50 laptops?

I would like 50 laptops.

It would be great if you could send us 50 laptops.

We are in need of 50 laptops.

Real Communication

Listen to the dialogue below and fill in the blanks.

1

A Good afternoon, Skiles Inc. How can I help you?

B Hello, this is Jamie Adams calling from Harber-Corwin. We're **1**_____ in purchasing some picture frames.

A Sure, I can help you with that. How many would you like to order?

B **2**_____ 75 units.

A Actually, we have an **3**_____ of 100 units.

B All right, 100 units should be no problem. Could we have a price estimate?

A You can find our price list on our website, but I can send you a **4**_____ by the end of the day.

B Great. Do you ship internationally? We're located in Alberta, Canada.

A Yes, we ship to Canada. The delivery will take approximately two to three weeks.

B Perfect. How can I proceed with the order?

A I'll email you an **5**_____ to fill out. As soon as we process your order, we'll send you an invoice with instructions for payment. Can I have your email address, please?

B Sure, it's jamie_ adams@harbercorwin.net

2

A Hello, is this Goodwin Supply?

B Yes, it is. My name is Alice. How can I help you?

A This is Todd calling from Perfect Grill. I'm calling **1**_____ our order number 52319.

B OK, let me pull that up on my computer... Yes, here it is. Unfortunately, it looks like one of the products you ordered is no longer in stock.

A Yes, we never received the ceramic mugs we ordered. I saw in your **2**_____ that item number 529 is quite similar. How many of those do you have in stock?

B Our warehouse is fully stocked with that item. How many would you like to purchase?

A Could you send 150 units **3**_____?

B Yes, not a problem. We can offer you the **4**_____, which includes a 5% discount.

A Great. Could we also have 50 units of item #399?

B The long-stem wine glasses? Certainly. I'll add that to your order. Is there anything else?

A No, that's everything. When can we expect to receive the **5**_____?

B As soon as the invoice is paid, we'll process your order and ship it out the same day. Your order will arrive within five business days.

A Great, thank you very much. Could you send the invoice by fax, please?

B Certainly. We have your fax number on file here.

A Listen to the dialogues again and answer the following questions.

1 How many units does Jamie Adams order?
   ⓐ 75　　　　　　　　　　　　ⓑ 100

2 When will Jamie Adams receive a price estimate?
   ⓐ by the end of the day　　　　ⓑ two to three weeks

3 Which item did Todd not receive?
   ⓐ ceramic mugs　　　　　　　ⓑ wine glasses

4 How does Todd want to receive the invoice?
   ⓐ email　　　　　　　　　　ⓑ fax

B Summarize the dialogues.

stock	bulk	place	invoice	order minimum	price estimate

In dialogue 1, Jamie Adams calls the supplier to 1_____ an order for picture frames. She wants to order 75 units, but there is an 2_____ of 100 units. She will receive a 3_____ by the end of the day, and the shipment will arrive in Alberta in two or three weeks.

In dialogue 2, Todd from Perfect Grill calls the supplier about an order. He did not receive the ceramic mugs he ordered, as they are out of 4_____. He orders a similar product instead and receives a discount for buying in 5_____. He also adds an order for wine glasses. The delivery will arrive within 5 days, and the 6_____ will be sent by fax.

Don't forget !

Delivery times are often given in terms of business days. A business day is any day that business are usually open, which includes all weekdays(Monday to Friday) except holidays.

Read what your client and supplier has to say and fill in the blanks with your own answers, using the hints on the side.

Practice A

Client	I would like to place an order for 30 boxes of ballpoint pens.
You	1 _____ ← Tell your client about the order minimum (50 boxes).
Client	All right, 50 boxes then. We're also going to need some staples.
You	2 _____ ← Ask how many they need.
Client	50 boxes of staples, as well.
You	No problem. 3 _____ ← Ask if your client has any other questions.
Client	How do I proceed with payment?
You	4 _____ ← Explain how you will send the invoice (email).

Practice B

Supplier	Hello, can I help you?
You	Yes, 1 _____ ← Explain that you want to place an order.
Supplier	What would you like to order?
You	2 _____ ← Say that you want 200 units of item number 291.
Supplier	All right, I've added that to your order. Is there anything else?
You	3 _____ ← Ask for a price estimate.
Supplier	The final price will be listed in your invoice.
You	4 _____ ← Ask about international shipping.
Supplier	Which country are you located in?
You	Our company is located in Germany.
Supplier	I will include a delivery quote in your invoice.
You	5 _____ ← Politely express thanks and say goodbye.

Review

A **Fill in the blanks with the missing words.**

update	confirm	shipped	reference

1 I'm calling in _____ to our order number 4522.

2 Can I have an _____ on my order number 531?

3 Your order will be _____ out tomorrow.

4 We'll _____ by email when your shipment has been sent.

B **Choose the correct word(s) or the phrase to complete each sentence.**

1 I am please to _____ receipt of your order number 9972.

   ⓐ invoice   ⓑ acknowledge   ⓒ place

2 We are interested in _____ 200 units.

   ⓐ purchasing   ⓑ shipping   ⓒ processing

3 When can we _____ to receive the shipment?

   ⓐ update   ⓑ confirm   ⓒ expect

C **Choose the expressions from the box to complete the dialogue in order.**

> ⓐ We are currently processing your order.
> ⓑ We'll confirm that with you when we receive your payment.
> ⓒ As soon as your order is processed, we'll send you the invoice by email.

A Hello, can I help you?

A Yes, this is Dennis from Carter Auto. Can I have an update on my order 2104?

B 1 _____

A OK. Can you please let me know the delivery date?

B 2 _____

A I see. And when can we make payment for the items?

B 3 _____

A Great, thank you very much.

B My pleasure. Have a nice day.

D **Choose the correct words to complete each sentence.**

1 We shipped (out/up) your order on Friday.

2 I'd like to (make/place) an order for 25 coffee tables.

3 You can find our catalog and price (book/list) online.

4 We will (confirm/check) your order by email.

E **Unscramble the words to make sentences.**

1 send / as / could / as / you / 75 units / soon / possible / ?

→ _____

2 buying / bulk / a / discount / there / for / is / in

→ _____

3 1029 / calling / I'm / in reference to / number / our / order

→ _____

4 in / stock / ? / do / how / you / many / have / books

→ _____

F **Fill in the blanks with the given words from the box.**

stock	catalog	internationally	wholesale	estimate

A Hello, is this QP Furniture Supply?

B Yes, it is. This is Ronald speaking. How can I help you today?

A I'd like to know more about the office chairs listed in your 1_____ .

B Sure, what would you like to know?

A How many do you have in 2_____? We're going to need quite a few.

B We have at least 300 in the warehouse ready for shipment. How many do you need?

A I'd like to place an order for 250. Do you offer a 3_____ price for those?

B Yes, we can provide a substantial price reduction for an order of that size.

A Great. Could you also send us 250 of the desk lamps?

B That shouldn't be a problem. I'll add it to your order.

A Do you ship 4_____?

A We can ship anywhere in Europe and North America.

B That's good to hear. Could we have a price 5_____ before finalizing the order?

A Of course. I'll get back to you with that by the end of the week.

Negotiating

Whether you are negotiating a business deal, a salary increase, or a job offer, negotiating is an important skill for success. In this unit, you will learn the essential expressions and vocabulary necessary for successfully completing a negotiation.

Warm up

A **Match each question 1–3 with two responses a–f.**

1 What do you think about our proposal?

2 How can we resolve this problem?

3 What is your proposal?

a We would be willing to compromise on the contract duration.

b We can give you 50 boxes for $800.

c It sounds reasonable to us.

d We recommend that you sign a 2-year contract with us.

e I have some reservations about the price.

f I'd like to present a counter-proposal.

B **When you negotiate a job offer, what do you say?**

flexible	with	reservations	problem	proposal

On the whole, your **1**_____ is reasonable. I don't see any **2**_____ with the duration of the contract, and I'm happy **3**_____ the vacation time and benefits. However, I have some **4**_____ about the salary. If you can be **5**_____ on this point, I would be willing to accept the offer.

Stating your position

At the start of the negotiation, these expressions will help you express your position.

We recommend that you start with a 1-year contract.
I can give you 20 boxes for $450.
Here is our best offer.
We are prepared to offer you a 3-year contract.
This is the salary we would like to offer you.
Your contract includes 14 days of paid time off.
Your contract includes a full benefits package.

Responding positively

These expressions are appropriate to express agreement with a point in the negotiation.

I'm happy with that.
I agree with you on that point.
I don't see any problem with that.
That's a fair suggestion.
I think your proposal/offer is reasonable.
That sounds great to us.
I couldn't agree more.

Responding negatively

It is difficult to express disagreement in a polite way. Use these expressions to help you.

I have some reservations about the salary.
I'm afraid we can't agree on the price per unit.
Some of your demands are a little unreasonable.
From my perspective, the price is still too high.
I'm afraid that doesn't work for me.
I take your point; however, we have to trust each other.
I'm afraid that's out of the question.
I'm afraid that those conditions are unacceptable.

Bargaining

These expressions will help you come to an agreement with your counterpart.

I'm willing to compromise on the price.
I'll see what I can do.
I'd like to present a counter-proposal.
We can be flexible in terms of contract duration.
I would prefer a longer contract.
In exchange for a longer contract, would you agree to less vacation time?
Would you consider increasing the base salary?

Closing

At the end of your negotiation, use these expressions to close the discussion.

I think we're ready to move forward.
Let me sleep on it.
I'm glad we've found some common ground.
I think we can both agree to these terms.
I'd like to stop and think about this for a little while.
Would you be willing to sign a contract right now?
I'm satisfied with this decision.

Circle the best response.

1 We'd like to offer you a 2-year contract.
A I'm willing to compromise on the salary. B Would you consider lowering the salary?
C I'm afraid that doesn't work for me.

2 I think we're ready to move forward.
A Yes, I think we can both agree to these terms. C I take your point.
B Yes, I would like to present a counter-proposal.

3 In exchange for a lower price, would you accept making a larger order?
A That's a fair suggestion. B I can be flexible in terms of salary.
C Would you be willing to sign a contract right now?

4 Let's go ahead and sign the contract.
A From my perspective, your offer is reasonable. C Here is our best offer.
B I'd like to stop and think about this for a while.

5 This is our best offer.
A I would prefer a similar proposal. B I'm satisfied with this decision.
C Some of your demands are a little unreasonable.

Real Business English

When negotiating, it is very important to be able to say "no" in a very polite and specific way. A common way to express disagreement is to use "I'm afraid" at the start of your statement. "Afraid," in this context, has nothing to do with fear; it has a meaning similar to "regretful."

e.g. **I'm afraid** I can't accept these terms.
I'm afraid we need to reconsider our goals.
I'm afraid this contract is unacceptable.
I'm afraid we cannot move forward with this negotiation.

Listen to the dialogue below and fill in the blanks.

1

A So Mr. Martinez, have you had time to review the job offer we sent you?

B I have, yes. I hope that we can discuss a few points.

A Sure, of course. What would you like to talk about?

B I have some **1**_____ about the benefits package. I didn't see anything about a pension program.

A Oh, that's mentioned briefly on page three. Your contract includes a full **2**_____ package, including enrollment in our pension program.

B All right, great. Would you consider increasing the base salary?

A I'm sorry, this is our **3**_____. You will, however, be eligible for a salary increase after 6 months, depending on your performance.

B I see. In exchange for a lower salary, would you agree to a higher overtime rate?

A That sounds like a **4**_____ suggestion. I will discuss it with the director.

B All right. I'm happy with everything else.

A If we can increase the overtime rate, would you be willing to sign a contract later this week?

B Yes, I think I'm ready to **5**_____.

2

A Thank you for coming. Mr. Sanders, we are **1**_____ to offer your company this proposal. Please take a few minutes to review it.

B OK, thank you, Ms. White... I notice here that the contract would be valid for only six months. At that point, the prices could be increased, is that right?

A Well, that's true, yes. Six months is our standard contract duration with a relatively new company such as yours.

B From my **2**_____, that puts us in an unstable position. I would prefer a longer contract. Would you consider extending it to two years?

A I'm afraid that's out of the question. We might be willing to **3**_____ on the price, but the contract duration is non-negotiable.

B Well, it's a shame we can't agree on this point. We may have to look elsewhere.

A Let's see if we can find some **4**_____. In exchange for extending your contract to one year, would you allow us to add some conditions? If the conditions are not met after six months, the contract will expire.

B Well, let me **5**_____. I would need to see the specifics on these conditions you mentioned.

A Yes, I understand. I'll have a revised contract drafted and sent to your office by the end of the week.

B Thank you. I'll be in touch.

A Listen to the dialogues again and answer the following questions.

1 What does Mr. Martinez have a question about?
   ⓐ the benefits package   ⓑ the contract duration

2 Does Mr. Martinez succeed in increasing the base salary?
   ⓐ yes   ⓑ no

3 What is the contract duration that Mr. Sanders prefers?
   ⓐ 18 months   ⓑ two years

4 Does Ms. White raise the prices in the contract?
   ⓐ yes   ⓑ no

B Summarize the dialogues.

refuses	duration	overtime	conditions	package	negotiating

In dialogue 1, Mr. Martinez discusses a job offer with a recruiter. He has a question about the pension program, and the recruiter explains that the contract includes a full benefits 1_____ . The recruiter 2_____ to adjust the salary but considers increasing the 3_____ rate.

In dialogue 2, Mr. Sanders discusses a contract offered to his company by Ms. White. Mr. Sanders would like the 4_____ of the contract to be increased from six months to two years. After some 5_____ , Ms. White agrees to extend the contract, but insists on adding some 6_____ to the contract.

Don't forget !

"Miss" refers to an unmarried woman.
"Mrs." (pronounced "missus") refers to a married woman.
Because it is considered impolite to assume (or ask about) whether a woman is married or unmarried, it is more polite to use the "Ms." (pronounced "mizz"). "Ms." can be used with any woman, regardless of age or marital status.

Read what your colleague and client has to say and fill in the blanks with your own answers, using the hints on the side.

Practice A

Colleague	Are you ready to sign the contract?	
You	Actually, 1_____	← Explain your reservations about the salary.
Colleague	From our perspective, this salary is suitable for your level of experience.	
You	2_____	← Explain that you understand, but ask for a higher salary.
Colleague	What salary do you feel would be appropriate?	
You	I would like the salary to be 20% higher than stated in this contract.	
Colleague	We may be able to increase the salary by 5%.	
You	3_____	← Explain that you would be satisfied with 15%.
Colleague	I'll see what I can do. What about the benefits package?	
You	4_____	← Respond positively.
Colleague	If we can increase the salary by 10%, would you be willing to sign?	
You	5_____	← Ask for some time to think about it.

Practice B

Client	I read your proposal, and I think it is quite reasonable.	
You	Great! 1_____	← Ask your client to sign the contract.
Client	Well, I have just one reservation. We would like deliveries twice a month instead of once a month.	
You	2_____	← Agree, but ask if she would be willing to pay more.
Client	That seems a bit unreasonable. Would you consider delivering every 3 weeks?	
You	3_____	← Respond positively.
Client	I'm glad we've found some common ground.	
You	4_____	← Close the deal.

A Fill in the blanks with the missing words.

| terms | prepared | flexible | unreasonable |

1 I think we can both agree to these _____ .

2 We can be _____ in terms of benefits.

3 Some of your demands are a little _____ .

4 We are _____ to offer you a new contract.

B Choose the correct word(s) or the phrase to complete each sentence.

1 I have some _____ about the delivery fee.

   ⓐ exchanges   ⓑ reservations   ⓒ perspectives

2 Let me _____ on it.

   ⓐ compromise   ⓑ agree   ⓒ sleep

3 That's a _____ suggestion.

   ⓐ fair   ⓑ high   ⓒ flexible

C Choose the expressions from the box to complete the dialogue in order.

> ⓐ I have some reservations about the vacation time.
> ⓑ OK, I'm happy with that.
> ⓒ I'm afraid that's out of the question.

A After much consideration, we would like to offer you a contract.

B That's great news. I hope we can work together.

A This is the salary we would like to offer you.

B 1 _____ Can I see the benefits package?

A Sure, here you are.

B 2 _____

A Oh? 10 days per year is our standard offer.

B I see. In my previous jobs, I have been offered 15 days of vacation.

A I take your point; however, 3 _____

B I understand. I will have to sleep on it.

D Choose the correct words to complete each sentence.

1 Would you be (ready/willing) to sign a contract right now?

2 Would you agree (to/with) a lower delivery fee?

3 From my (perspective/condition), the salary is a little low.

4 Our offer includes a full benefits (proposal/package).

E Unscramble the words to make sentences.

1 afraid / agree / the / I'm / fee / on / we / can't / delivery

→_____

2 question / the / afraid / out / I'm / of / that's

→_____

3 on / to / willing / I'm / time / the / vacation / compromise

→_____

4 forward / think / we're / I / to / ready / move

→_____

F Fill in the blanks with the given words from the box.

perspective	terms	reservations	compromise	consider

A I'm glad we've found some common ground.

B Yes, I think we're ready to move forward.

A Well, I still have some 1_____. This software is quite complicated, and I would like to include training for my employees as part of the deal.

B I agree with you on that point.

A Would you 2_____ conducting a two-day seminar for my staff? We have 15 employees.

B I don't see any problem with that. We can provide that for $1500.

A From my 3_____, that seems a little high.

B I'm willing to 4_____ on the price. How about $1200?

A I'm happy with that.

A Great, I think we can both agree to those 5_____.

B I'll amend the contract and have it sent to your office.

A I'll review it and send you a signed copy by the end of the week. It's a pleasure doing business with you.

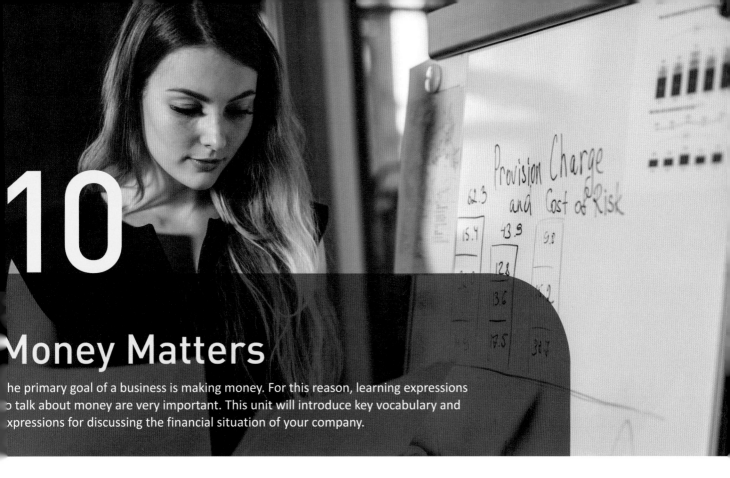

10

Money Matters

The primary goal of a business is making money. For this reason, learning expressions to talk about money are very important. This unit will introduce key vocabulary and expressions for discussing the financial situation of your company.

Warm up

A Match each question 1–3 with two responses a–f.

1 Why are we losing so much money?

2 How have you been so successful?

3 What do you predict for next quarter?

a Sales are likely to fluctuate month to month.

b We took a loss on the Millstone account.

c The whole industry is experiencing a recession.

d We expect an increase in revenue.

e We are able to keep overhead very low.

f Our profit margins are among the highest in the industry.

B When you describe a sales graph, what do you say?

from	to	and	by

As you can see here, overall sales jumped 1_____ ten percent between November 2_____ December. Sales of women's clothing, in particular, rose 3_____ $40,000 4_____ $45,000, and this number is expected to reach $50,000 by the end of the year.

Talking about money

These are some of the most common expressions for discussing money issues at a company.

We need to increase profit and reduce expenses.

Sales revenue has increased by 15%.

Our monthly revenue was highest in December.

We can reduce our overhead by moving to a smaller building.

What is our profit margin on this product?

We cannot pay this month due to cash flow problems.

The company has a lot of assets, but not much cash on hand.

What is the sales forecast for February?

The balance sheet shows that we need to increase revenue.

What is our marketing budget for next quarter?

Money trends

When talking about changes and trends, these descriptive verbs are useful. As you will see, they are great for describing graphs.

Profits have declined by 30% in the last year.

Sales are projected to drop by 10% after Christmas.

We expect expenses to level off by the end of this quarter.

Sales remained steady throughout the first quarter.

Revenue typically fluctuates throughout the year.

Profits have risen by 10% compared to last month.

Sales usually jump in mid-November.

Financial success

These expressions are used when a company's financial situation is positive.

This publishing house is one of the most successful in the industry.

We have remained profitable despite the poor economy.

This will be our most lucrative project so far.

The early sales figures are very promising.

We hope to outperform our competition this year.

We have remained competitive while cutting expenses.

Financial problems

We use these expressions when a company is struggling financially.

Unfortunately, that company went bankrupt last year.

That company is likely to go out of business by the end of the year.

We really can't afford to make such a large purchase.

We need to be thrifty for the next few months.

Our company has a lot of debt.

The industry is in the middle of a recession.

I'm afraid we'll have to take a loss on this project.

We've been operating in the red for the last six months.

Circle the best response.

1   Your company seems to be struggling a little.
A Yes, we went bankrupt last year.   B Yes, we're currently in the red.
C Yes, we are quite competitive.

2   What does the balance sheet show?
A Our expenses are too high.   B The project is very promising.
C We are not outperforming the competition.

3   Why are you going out of business?
A Our sales department is too competitive.   B We need to be very thrifty.
C The company just has too much debt.

4   Are profits going up?
A Yes, they are fluctuating a lot.   B Yes, they are expected to level off soon.
C Yes, they have jumped 15% from last month.

5   How can we increase profits?
A We should reduce our overhead.   B We should reduce our assets.
C We should reduce our forecast.

Real Business English

When talking about trends, you can add adverbs (steadily, significantly, sharply, dramatically, suddenly, etc.) to describe the change more specifically. Many of the verbs we use to describe trends (decline, drop, rise, jump, etc.) can be used as nouns as well. It's common to use them with "experience" or sentences with "there is."

e.g.   Profits have declined **sharply** since last summer.
Sales are rising **steadily**.
Expenses fluctuate **significantly** from month to month.

We **experienced** a 10% **jump** in sales from November to December.
There was a 20% **drop** in revenue.
We will **experience** a sharp **decline** in book sales this quarter.
There will be a significant **rise** in expenses next year.

Listen to the dialogue below and fill in the blanks.

1

A Hi, Fernanda. How was your meeting with the director?

B Hello, Chad. It went really well. She's very happy with our progress this quarter.

A Yeah? What did she say?

B She said our department is one of the most **1**_____ in the company.

A Oh, that's great. Did you show her our **2**_____ for next month? I think it's really promising.

B I did, yes. She is a little worried about our expenses, however, as they've risen significantly over the last several months.

A That's true. But they should **3**_____ this quarter.

B I hope so. If we want to stay competitive, we need to maintain our **4**_____.

A Agreed. Did you explain our cash flow issue? If we had more **5**_____, we could place bigger orders and save some money on materials.

B She said she would work on it. We need to clear some of our debt first.

A That makes sense. In any case, I'm glad she's noticed how successful we've been.

B Agreed. Things are really looking up!

2

A Felix, could you present the quarterly sales report for the publishing department, please?

B Yes, I would be happy to. If you'll take a look at the graph here, you'll see that we're experiencing a **1**_____ in textbook sales.

A How is it, then, that profits have remained steady?

B Well, sales of children's books have risen by 20%, so we've been able to stay **2**_____.

A I see. Is there a reason that textbook sales have been so weak?

B The textbook industry as a whole is experiencing a recession. Students are moving toward ebooks and textbook rentals. We have also shifted a lot of our marketing budget to other areas, mainly literature and self-help books.

A I see. Textbooks are so costly to produce, we can't really afford to **3**_____ on them. Is there any way to reduce expenses?

B We are looking at ways to improve the **4**_____ to compensate for the drop in sales.

A I'd like to hear some of those ideas. We'll meet next week to talk about that. What is the forecast for next quarter?

B We expect to see a **5**_____ in profits, especially as the holiday season approaches.

A Excellent. Thank you, Felix.

B My pleasure.

A **Listen to the dialogues again and answer the following questions.**

1 What is Fernanda's director worried about?
   ⓐ sales   ⓑ expenses

2 What issue does Chad mention?
   ⓐ profit margin   ⓑ cash flow

3 What type of books have been the most lucrative?
   ⓐ children's books   ⓑ textbooks

4 How is the sales forecast for next quarter?
   ⓐ positive   ⓑ negative

B **Summarize the dialogues.**

debt	expenses	reduce	forecast	textbook	profits

In dialogue 1, Chad asks Fernanda about her meeting with the director. The director is
satisfied with their sales 1_____, but she is worried about their 2_____. Chad
asks about the cash flow issue, and the director said she would work on it, but the current
level of 3_____ is a problem.

In dialogue 2, Felix presents the sales report to his manager. He explains that textbooks sales
have declined, but 4_____ are strong because of the success of children's books. Felix
explains why 5_____ sales have been weak, and he promises to find ways to
6_____ expenses. He expects profits to go up next quarter.

Don't forget !

When making predictions, or when you're not 100% sure about something, it is important to use
"hedging" language. This shows the listener your level of certainty. For example,

Sales **should** improve next month.
Sales **are likely to** improve next month.
Sales **will probably** improve next month.

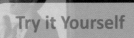
Read what your colleague has to say and fill in the blanks with your own answers, using the hints on the side.

Practice A

Colleague	Congratulations on the success of your new company!
You	Thank you! However, 1 _____ ← Say that you are not profitable yet.
Colleague	That's common for a new business. How are your sales?
You	2 _____ ← Describe the increase in sales last month.
Colleague	Oh, good! Any predictions for next quarter?
You	Well, 3 _____ ← Describe your sales forecast.
Colleague	That's great to hear. Are you struggling with anything?
You	4 _____ ← Explain the problem (overhead).

Practice B

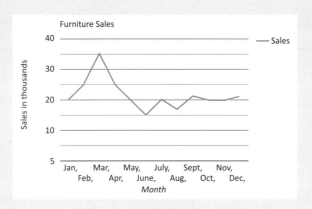

Colleague	Tell me what happened from January to March.
You	1 _____
Colleague	OK, and what happened in the second quarter?
You	2 _____
Colleague	Can you describe the sales figures in the third quarter?
You	3 _____
Colleague	And how about during the final quarter of the year?
You	4 _____

A Fill in the blanks with the missing words.

overhead	assets	promising	thrifty

1 We have more _____ than we had last year.

2 The sales forecast is quite _____.

3 We are being _____ because of our low budget.

4 Our _____ is very low, which is a good sign.

B Choose the correct word(s) or the phrase to complete each sentence.

1 The CEO is happy with the _____ in profits.
   ⓐ drop   ⓑ jump   ⓒ decline

2 We are struggling to _____ the competition.
   ⓐ fluctuate   ⓑ outperform   ⓒ afford

3 We will probably go _____ by the end of the year.
   ⓐ lucrative   ⓑ recession   ⓒ bankrupt

C Choose the expressions from the box to complete the dialogue in order.

> ⓐ We're trying to reduce expenses as much as possible.
> ⓑ We're having some issues with cash flow.
> ⓒ We'll go out of business if we don't turn things around.

A Your business seems to be struggling a bit.

B Yes, that's for sure. **1** _____

A Oh, that is serious. What's going on? Is it a debt problem?

B No, not exactly. **2** _____

A I see. That's a pretty common problem for new companies.

B Yes, but I started this company five years ago. We should be out of the red by now.

A I agree. How do you plan to fix it?

B **3** _____

A That's easier said than done.

B Agreed. I hope we don't have to lay off any staff.

D Choose the correct words to complete each sentence.

1 The industry is going through a (recession/drop).

2 We need to reduce our (overhead/revenue).

3 Prices have leveled (up/off) recently.

4 We need to raise prices to be more (profitable/promising).

E Unscramble the words to make sentences.

1 we / to / trying / going / avoid / bankrupt / are

→ _____

2 is / one / our / projects / of / most / this / lucrative

→ _____

3 year / this / have / profits / by / 10% / risen

→ _____

4 by / improve / we / expenses / our / cutting / can / profit margin

→ _____

F Fill in the blanks with the given words from the box.

jumped	overhead	fluctuate	dropped	cash on hand

A Let's take a look at our month revenue from last year.

B All right, I have the graph here.

A You can see that revenue 1_____ significantly in August, so that's something we want to avoid this year.

B I see your point. But the final quarter was strong, especially in November, when revenue 2_____ by 15%.

A Yes, I just don't want the numbers to 3_____ so much. We need a steady revenue stream.

B I agree. What about cash flow? If we had more 4_____, we could make bigger orders and get better deals from our suppliers.

A We can liquidate some of our assets, which will free up some more cash.

B I think that's a good idea. Anything else?

A Have you thought about ways to reduce our 5_____?

A Well, we could consider moving our offices to a different building.

B This neighborhood is quite expensive, but I think the location is perfect.

A That's a good point. I'll look around at buildings nearby.

11
Complaining and Apologizing

Sometimes people and companies make mistakes. One of the most important skills in business is discussing and resolving problems in a polite manner. This unit will teach you the expressions that English speakers use to make complaints and mediate conflict.

Warm up

A **Match each question 1–3 with two responses a–f.**

1 What seems to be the problem?

2 How are you going to resolve this?

3 I'm very disappointed with this product.

a I realize this has been an inconvenience to you.

b I would like to offer you a full refund.

c I'm having a hard time accessing the digital content.

d We can offer you an in-store exchange for that item.

e There's a slight problem with our order.

f I understand that this is frustrating for you.

B **When you apologize to an angry customer, what do you say?**

for	full	bringing	take	submit

Thank you for 1_____ this to our attention. I understand this is frustrating for you, and we 2_____ full responsibility 3_____ the problem. It appears there was a misunderstanding with our production facility. We would like to offer you a 4_____ refund, and we ask that you please 5_____ a formal complaint through our website.

Complaining

These expressions are useful for expressing your complaints.

How can I help you?
- I would like to report an issue.
- I would like to make a complaint.
- I would like to inform you that our delivery has still not arrived.
- I'm calling to complain about your sales representative.

What seems to be the problem?
- I'm having a hard time understanding the training materials.
- I'm afraid there's a problem with our new equipment.
- I'm disappointed with the service I received.
- There's a slight problem with our order.

If you can't fulfill the order on time, I'll have to find a new supplier.

Apologizing

Use one of these expressions to apologize to a disappointed customer or company.

Thank you for bringing this to our attention.
There seems to be some kind of mix-up.
It appears there was a misunderstanding.
There seems to have been some miscommunication.
I'm afraid there's been an oversight on our part.
I'm sorry to hear that the item is defective.
You can submit a formal complaint on our website.
I sincerely apologize for the inconvenience.
On behalf of Jameson Co., I offer my sincerest apologies.
We take full responsibility for the problem.

Offering compensation

After apologizing, use these expressions to explain how you will solve the problem.

I would like to know what you are going to do about this.
- We would like to compensate you for your trouble.
- We would like to offer you a full refund.
- We would like to offer you a discount on your next purchase.
- We can offer you an in-store exchange for that item.

Dealing with frustration

We use these expressions when a company is struggling financially.

You have every reason to be upset.
I understand this is frustrating for you.
I realize this has been an inconvenience to you.
I promise we will do everything we can to solve the problem.
I understand where you are coming from.

Circle the best response.

1 I'm afraid there's a problem with our order.
   A I sincerely apologize for the inconvenience.   B I would like to make a complaint.
   C I'm calling to complain about the quality of these items.

2 I would like a full refund.
   A I'm disappointed with the service I received.   B There is problem with our order.
   C We can offer you an in-store exchange.

3 I am extremely frustrated with the whole process.
   A I'm disappointed with the service I received.   B We'd like to submit a formal complaint.
   C I promise we will do everything we can to solve the problem.

4 How can I help you?
   A We can offer you an in-store exchange.   B I'm calling to complain about our order.
   C I'm afraid there's been an oversight on our part.

5 Our new fax machines are not working at all.
   A On behalf of QR Supply, I offer my sincerest apologies.   C Thank you for calling.
   B I would like to know what you are going to do about this.

Real Business English

When apologizing, it is common to use indirect or passive language, rather than being direct. This allows you to protect the person or department that made the mistake. For example, you should avoid saying this:

Our marketing department made a mistake.
The sales team forgot to read your email.
I sent you the wrong document.

Instead, you should say it indirectly:

There was a mix-up in the marketing department.
There seems to have been some miscommunication with the sales team.
The wrong document was sent to you.

Listen to the dialogue below and fill in the blanks.

1

A Hello, how can I help you today?

B Hi. I'm calling to make a **1**_____.

A Oh, what seems to be the problem?

B I bought a pair of boots from your online shop, and the actual product did not match the description on the website.

A Thank you for bringing this to **2**_____. Can you tell me which boots you purchased?

B The knee-high work boots. I ordered the dark brown, and the boots I received are much lighter than I expected.

A I'm very sorry to hear that. Can you give me your order number?

B It's 51399.

A OK, it appears there was some kind of **3**_____ with our distributer. We would like to offer you **4**_____ for that item. We will send you a shipping label, so you can send them back.

B That seems like a lot of work on my part. This is extremely frustrating!

A You have **5**_____ to be upset. We take full responsibility for the mistake, and we would like to offer you a 25% discount on your next purchase by way of apology.

B Well, thank you for your help.

A Thank you for calling. I hope you have a nice day.

2

A Hello, JC Supply, this is Sheila speaking. How can I help you?

B Hello, this is Pedro Romano from Bradley Meyers. **1**_____ there is a problem with the fax machines we received.

A I'm very sorry to **2**_____. What seems to be the problem?

B They are simply not turning on. We plug them in and nothing happens.

A I see. I'm sorry to hear that the items are **3**_____. I'll arrange for a technician to visit your office and investigate the problem.

B Well, I called last week and was promised the same thing.

A Let me open your account here, just a moment… OK, it looks like there was some **4**_____ with the technician. I'm very sorry about that.

B This is really causing problems for us. We already got rid of our old machines.

A I completely understand where you're **5**_____. I am contacting the technician right now, and he will be there by the end of the day.

B Thank you for taking care of this.

A You're very welcome.

A Listen to the dialogues again and answer the following questions.

1 What is the problem with the boots that the customer ordered?
   ⓐ size   ⓑ color

2 What does the customer service representative offer?
   ⓐ an in-store exchange   ⓑ a full refund

3 Is this the first time Pedro Romano has called about the problem?
   ⓐ no   ⓑ yes

4 Who will visit the office?
   ⓐ the technician   ⓑ Sheila

B Summarize the dialogues.

promises	technician	complain	offers	fax machines	color

In dialogue 1, a customer is calling to 1 _____ about some boots that he ordered online. The 2 _____ of the boots did not match the online description. The customer service representative explains the process of exchanging the boots. The customer is upset, and the customer service representative 3 _____ a 25% discount.

In dialogue 2, Pedro Romano calls an office supply company to explain that the new 4 _____ he ordered are not working. Sheila apologizes, explains that there was some miscommunication with the 5 _____ , and 6 _____ that the technician will arrive today.

Don't forget !

As a customer service representative, you often need to gather personal information from the customer. Be careful to ask for this information politely using the following expressions.

Can you give me your order number?
Could you tell me your full name, please?

Read what your supplier and customer has to say and fill in the blanks with your own answers, using the hints on the side.

Practice A

Supplier	How can I help you?	
You	Hello. 1_____	⟵ Say that you have a complaint.

Supplier	What seems to be the problem?	
You	2_____	⟵ Describe the problem with your delivery.

Supplier	Can you tell me your order number, please?
You	Yes, the order number is 59910.

Supplier	Oh, it appears there was some kind of mix-up with the delivery service.	
You	3_____	⟵ Ask what they are going to do to solve it.

Supplier	We can offer you an in-store exchange or a full refund.	
You	4_____	⟵ Ask for a refund.

Supplier	Yes, we'll process your refund right away.	
You	5_____	⟵ Thank your supplier and say goodbye.

Practice B

Customer	I'm calling to make a complaint.	
You	1_____	⟵ Ask what the problem is.

Customer	The phone I received is not working properly.	
You	2_____	⟵ Apologize about the defective product.

Customer	I read positive reviews about it, so I'm very disappointed.	
You	3_____	⟵ Calm your customer down.

Customer	Can you give me a refund?	
You	4_____	⟵ Offer an in-store exchange and a discount.

A **Fill in the blanks with the missing words.**

apologize	reason	disappointed	attention

1 You have every _____ to be upset.

2 I sincerely _____ for the inconvenience.

3 Thank you for bringing this to our _____.

4 I'm _____ with the product I received.

B **Choose the correct word(s) or the phrase to complete each sentence.**

1 I would like to _____ you that the item is defective.
   ⓐ submit   ⓑ bring   ⓒ inform

2 I understand this is _____ for you.
   ⓐ compensate   ⓑ frustrating   ⓒ disappointed

3 I'm afraid there's been some _____ on our part.
   ⓐ responsibility ⓑ oversight   ⓒ complaint

C **Choose the expressions from the box to complete the dialogue in order.**

ⓐ Thank you for bringing this to our attention.
ⓑ We will send them out right away.
ⓒ What seems to be the problem?

A Hello, how can I help you?

B I'm calling because there's a slight problem with our order.

A I'm sorry to hear that. 1 _____

B We ordered 20 boxes, but our delivery contained only 18 boxes.

A 2 _____ There seems to be some kind of mix-up.

B When can we receive the other two boxes?

A 3 _____ You will receive them by tomorrow afternoon.

B Thank you very much.

A You're very welcome. I apologize for the inconvenience.

D Choose the correct words to complete each sentence.

1 We would like to (compensate/apologize) you for your trouble.

2 I'm sorry to hear that the item is (misunderstanding/defective).

3 We take full (refund/responsibility) for the problem.

4 I completely understand (where/how) you are coming from.

E Unscramble the words to make sentences.

1 formal / submit / website / on / you / a / complaint / our / can

→_____

2 the / disappointed / received / I / with / I'm / service

→_____

3 you / a discount / purchase / on / we / next / offer / would like to / your

→_____

4 to be / reason / upset / have / you / every

→_____

F Fill in the blanks with the given words from the box.

sincerest	seems	upset	complaint	complaint

A Hello, how can I help you?

B I'm calling to 1_____ about your sales representative.

A I'm sorry to hear that. Can you give me the person's name, please?

B His name is Fred Banks.

A And what 2_____ to be the problem?

B We placed an order with him, but the delivery never arrived. And we have been unable to contact him for a week.

A On behalf of Trading Inc., I offer my 3_____ apologies. There seems to have been some miscommunication.

B We would like to have a different sales representative assigned to us immediately.

A You have every reason to be 4_____ . We will assign a new representative right away.

A And what about Mr. Banks?

B I would like to ask you to submit a formal 5_____ on our website so that we can follow up.

A I will. Thank you for your help. Goodbye.

12

Business Correspondence

owadays, corresponding with the English written word, especially by email, is an essential art of doing international business. If you know some formal business expressions to use n your writing, you'll be able to communicate in a much more professional manner.

Warm up

A **Match each question 1–3 with two responses a–f.**

1 How do you begin a formal business email?

2 How do you end a formal business email?

3 How do you begin an informal email?

a What's up, guys? I have good news.

b If you have any questions or concerns, feel free to email, call, or text me.

c Dear Liu, Thank you for contacting me.

d Hello Allen, I hope everything is going well.

e Let me know if you have any questions regarding this matter.

f You know what Wanda? Good news!

B **When you write an email to your coworker, what do you write?**

know	discount	hello	thank	problem

1_____ Jacob,

2_____ you for your quick response to the urgent memo. I think Sofia has found a solution to the 3_____ with the Havertown account. We'll process the order again and give them a 25% 4_____ to make them happy. In the meantime, I was hoping you could make sure the other orders that went out this week went smoothly. Please let me 5_____ ASAP.

Thanks,

Beverly

Formal email and letter introductions

You should always include a greeting, gratitude for previous correspondence and/or expressions to catch up, and the purpose/topic of your email.

Greetings (first name in most cases, but title and surname in very formal situations)

- Dear Marcus,/Hello Dr. Nguyen,

Gratitude/catching up

- Thank you so much for getting back to me.
- Thank you for your quick reply.
- How are you?
- I hope everything is going well.

Purpose/topic

- I'm writing to let you know that we're interested in making a large order next month.
- I wanted to inform you that we are very pleased with the products and we want to place another order.
- I'm emailing you to ask if you'll be able to meet next month.

Informal email introductions

For business emails sent to coworkers, colleagues or even customers that you know well, it's more appropriate to use informal expressions. Using very formal language could sound too cold.

Greetings (first name is fine in most cases)

- Hey Michelle,/Hi Stewart,

Gratitude/catching up

- Thanks for getting back to me.
- Thanks for your quick reply.
- How are things?
- I hope all is well.

Purpose/topic

- I just wanted to tell you that we have a meeting at 4 p.m.
- Just to let you know, we're having cocktails together at 5 p.m.
- About the meeting. I'm sorry if I was a bit rude.

Formal email and letter conclusions

Conclusions should typically include an expression of gratitude, an expectation/instruction, and a final farewell.

Gratitude

- Thank you very much again for hosting last week.
- I very much appreciate your quick response.

Expectation/instruction

- Please let me know if you have any questions.
- If you have any questions, please feel free to ask.
- I look forward to meeting you in person.
- I will let you know if there are changes to the schedule.
- I would greatly appreciate your feedback on this.

Farewell

- I'll see you soon,/Best wishes,/Yours faithfully,/Sincerely,/ Regards,

Informal email conclusions

Use these expressions for coworkers, colleagues, and customers you know well.

Gratitude
- Thanks again for everything.
- I'm glad you joined us for lunch.

Expectation/instruction
- Let me know if you need anything else.
- I'll get back to you soon.
- Hope you can make it to the team dinner tomorrow night.

Farewell
- See you,/Best,/Cheers,

Quiz   **Circle the best response.**

1   Which *formal* expression fits this email introduction?

_____ Professor Rodriguez,

Thank you so much for your quick reply. It is my understanding that the date for grade submission was the 14th of this month, so it will be important for us to discuss any failed students beforehand.

A What's up   B Hey   C Hello

2   Which *informal* expression fits this email introduction?

Hey Maria,

_____. Just to let you know, I can't make it to the meeting this afternoon.

A I hope all is well.   B Thank you so much for your previous correspondence.
C I very much appreciate your attention concerning this matter.

Real Business English

It's common to include a "call to action" toward the end of your email. A "call to action" gives the reader an instruction about what they should after reading your email. For example, if you are making a complaint to another company, you might write, "Please correct this mistake as soon as possible." You can also be more indirect by writing, "I look forward to your response."

e.g.   Let me know when the situation is resolved.
Please contact me by the end of the week.
Please discuss this issue with the marketing team and let me know your decision.

Listen to the emails below and fill in the blanks.

1

> 1_____ Kofi Banta,
>
> Thank you so much for getting 2_____ regarding your company's new R&D report. Your information was quite useful. I'm 3_____ you now to let you know that our company is very interested in a joint venture after much consideration. 4_____ you and your team to our office here in Los Angeles early next month to discuss the details in person. We'd love to cover your flight and accommodation as well.
>
> 5_____ very much again for your excellent report. 6_____ hearing from you very soon.
>
> Thank you,
>
> Marsha Brady

2

> 1_____ Amanda,
>
> I hope 2_____. Just 3_____, we have a visit from the CEO coming next month. Linda told me that we need to start prepping a bunch of things. Oh, and about the TPS reports, 4_____ you get them to Mike before the end of the day.
> I'll get back to you soon about the preparations for the CEO visit.
>
> 5_____,
>
> Courtney

3

> 1_____ Courtney,
>
> Okay. 2_____. I think we can have all of that ready before he gets here. And don't worry, I just sent my TPS reports this morning.
>
> Thanks,
>
> Amanda

A **Read the emails again and answer the following questions.**

1 What is Marsha happy about?
ⓐ Kofi's company's R&D report   ⓑ the joint venture

2 What does Marsha's company want in the future?
ⓐ more R&D reports   ⓑ for Kofi and his team to visit

3 What does Amanda's coworkers need to prepare for?
ⓐ the TPS reports   ⓑ the CEO's coming visit

4 What did Amanda do in response to Courtney's mail?
ⓐ She sent the TPS reports.   ⓑ She made all the things ready before CEO's visit.

B **Summarize the dialogues.**

joint venture	submit	come	visit	R&D	invite

In email 1, Marsha writes to Kofi to express her gratitude for the **1**_____ report. She's so happy about the report that she wants to **2**_____ members of Kofi's company to **3**_____ to L.A. to discuss a possible **4**_____.

In emails 2 and 3, Courtney informs Amanda of the CEO's **5**_____ next month and reminds her to **6**_____ the TPS reports to Mike today. She'll tell Amanda more about the visit later. Amanda responds by telling her that she agrees about the preparations and that she's already turned in the TPS reports.

Don't forget !

Modern expressions like "OMG" (oh my god) and "LOL" (laugh out loud) are only for texting informally with your friends and are NOT okay in any kind of business email, neither formal nor informal. For informal and brief business emails, it's fine to use common classics like "ASAP" (as soon as possible) and "FYI" (for your information).

Practice A

Write your own formal introduction and conclusion to this email. You only have the body and pieces of the intro and conclusion of the email to give you clues. Study the key expressions closely and use them here!

1_____ Mr. Jenkins,

2_____ regarding next month's conference. 3_____ the schedule will be very demanding, so I thought I'd give you an overview.

There will be small presentations all morning from 8 a.m. to 12 p.m. The conference will then give a buffet lunch in the main hall. After that, participants will attend various workshops between 1 p.m. and 3 p.m. You, Mr. Jenkins, will of course be our plenary speaker, so you will give the final speech in the main hall at 3 p.m. sharp.

4_____ volunteering your time as a speaker. If you have any questions, 5_____ I will let you know if there are changes to the schedule.

Best wishes,

Michael Johnson

Practice B

Write your own informal introduction and conclusion to this email. You only have the body and pieces of the intro and conclusion of the email to give you clues.

1_____ Biff,

2_____ Just to let you know, we have an emergency meeting at 4 p.m. today. There's been another issue with the Sao Paolo account. They said that they were billed too much again, so we need to fix problems with accounting.

3_____ you're back from paternity leave so that you can fix these problems. 4_____ you have any questions.

5_____ ,

Marty

Review

A **Fill in the blanks with the missing words.**

> things   inform   appreciate   reply

1 Thanks for your quick _____.

2 I just wanted to _____ you that we're really happy with your latest deal.

3 How are _____?

4 I very much _____ your feedback.

B **Choose the correct word(s) or the phrase to complete each sentence.**

1 If you have any questions, please feel free to _____.

   ⓐ tell   ⓑ ask   ⓒ send

2 I'll _____ to you soon.

   ⓐ get back   ⓑ call   ⓒ contact

3 I would _____ appreciate it if you could help out the marketing team.

   ⓐ super   ⓑ very   ⓒ greatly

C **Choose the expressions from the box to complete the email in order.**

> ⓐ See you soon.
> ⓑ Hey Mary,
> ⓒ Thanks for getting back to me so quickly.

1 _____

2 _____ I agree with your ideas on the product launch. We'll discuss it at tomorrow's meeting. Also, I think we should try to bring up the issues we've been having with the HR department. A lot of us feel uncomfortable with the new rules, so I think we should bring it up to Mr. Thompson.

By the way, are we still on for lunch tomorrow, or will you be busy with those new clients?

3 _____

Abdul-Aziz

D **Choose the correct words to complete each sentence.**

1 It is my (knowledge/understanding) that we get paid on the first of every month.

2 I (hope/wish) everything is going well.

3 I (looking/look) forward to our meeting tomorrow.

4 Thanks (for/to) getting back to me.

E **Unscramble the words to make sentences.**

1 let you / on the 31st / that / writing to / I'm / know / is / the conference

→ _____

2 my / quick / email / your / thanks / to / reply / for

→ _____

3 questions / if / free / feel / have / you / to / any / ask

→ _____

4 will let / the meeting / I / will be / you / tomorrow / know / what time

→ _____

F **Fill in the blanks with the given words from the box.**

let you know	appreciate	inform	again	reply

Hello Mrs. Yuen,

Thank you for your quick 1_____ regarding our mistaken order. We 2_____ it very much. However, I'm writing to 3_____ you that we have chosen a new supplier. We need a consistent supplier. You have been so kind to us Mrs. Yuen, and we know it's not your fault personally, but please let your superiors know why we're discontinuing our account.

Thank you very much 4_____ for your personal attention. I will 5_____ if we need your services in the future.

Regards,

James Madison

Answer Keys

01 Meeting New Colleagues

Warm up **A** 1 b, c 2 d, f 3 a, e

B Hello, my **1** <u>name</u> is Joon Choi, and I work in the electronics **2** <u>department</u>. I work **3** <u>for</u> Dronix **4** <u>as</u> an electrical engineer. We **5** <u>manufacture</u> custom computer parts for large companies.

Quiz 1 A 2 C 3 C 4 B 5 A

Real Communication

1

A	Hi Barry, long time no see! How's it going?
B	Jeremy, hi! Yes, it's been a while. I'm doing well. **1** <u>How are things</u> with you? I think you were working as an assistant the last time I saw you.
A	Yeah, that's right. I actually moved to a new company. I'm working at Cardtop now.
B	Oh, that's impressive! I've heard good things about Cardtop. **2** <u>What do you do</u> there?
A	I'm working as an account manager. I just have a few **3** <u>clients</u> for now, but it's going really well.
B	That's fantastic! I actually got out of the **4** <u>finance industry</u>.
A	Is that right? What are you doing now?
B	I'm working in marketing. It was a pretty big shift, but I'm getting the hang of it.
A	That sounds interesting. My cousin is in marketing actually. Which company?
B	Have you heard of Adslant? We're a relatively **5** <u>new company</u>. I'm working as a researcher there.
A	Well, I hope you're liking it. I think marketing really suits you.

2

A	Hi, are you here for the conference?
B	Yes. I hope I'm not too early. The first speaker is at 9:00, right?
A	Yes, that's right. Most people are still out in the lobby getting breakfast. My name is Kelly Stewart. It's a pleasure to meet you.
B	**1** <u>The pleasure is all mine</u>. I'm Tim Robbins. So what do you do, Ms. Stewart?
A	Oh, you can call me Kelly. I work in the product development department at Metrice. What about you?
B	I work for a **2** <u>startup</u> as a coder. We design security solutions for app developers.
A	That sounds really interesting! Where are you located?
B	Our headquarters are in New York, but I work **3** <u>remotely</u>. I live really close to here, actually, just a 10-minute drive.
A	Well, that's convenient. You don't have to worry about hotels and transportation, I guess.
B	Exactly. Was it a long flight for you?
A	No, not too bad. My office is in San Jose. We **4** <u>flew in</u> yesterday, so I was able to get a decent night's sleep.
B	Oh, it looks like they're getting ready to start. Let me give you my card.
A	OK, great, and here's mine. Feel free to **5** <u>contact</u> me anytime.

A 1 b 2 b 3 a 4 a

B In dialogue A, Barry and Jeremy are old friends who meet after a long time. Jeremy used to be an **1** <u>assistant</u>, but now he's working for a new company as an **2** <u>account manager</u>. Barry has left the finance industry and is now working in marketing as a **3** <u>researcher</u>. His company, Adslant, is relatively new.

In dialogue B, Kelly and Tim meet at the start of a conference. They introduce themselves and talk about their jobs. Kelly works in the product development department, and Tim works as a coder for a **4** <u>startup</u>. Tim works **5** <u>remotely</u> and lives nearby, and Kelly took a plane from San Jose, where her company is located. They exchange **6** <u>contact information</u>.

Try it Yourself

Practice A Sample Answers

Colleague	Hello! My name is Samantha Corbin. Nice to meet you.
You	1 Hello, I'm Jason Kim. It's a pleasure to meet you, too.
Colleague	Do you mind if I call you by your first name?
You	No, not at all. 2 What do you do for work, Samantha?
Colleague	I work as an intern at Cortech.
You	Oh, I haven't heard of that company.
Colleague	We specialize in providing energy solutions for factories.
You	Oh, that sounds really interesting.
Colleague	How about you? What do you do?
You	3 I'm an assistant manager at a large technology company.
Colleague	That sounds very interesting. Well, it was a pleasure meeting you.
You	The pleasure is all mine. 4 Can I give you my card?

Practice B Sample Answers

Colleague	Hi, there! Good to see you again!
You	Oh, hello Michael! 1 How are things with you?
Colleague	I can't complain. What about you? I heard you're at a new company now.
You	Yes, that's right. 2 We sell medical equipment to hospitals.
Colleague	That sounds really exciting! What do you do there?
You	3 I'm working as a sales manager.
Colleague	That's really great, congratulations. I'm late for a meeting. I'll talk to you soon.
You	OK, Michael, we'll catch up later.

Review

A 1 contact 2 solutions 3 department 4 field

B 1 b 2 a 3 a

C 1 c 2 a 3 B

D 1 pleasure 2 established 3 in 4 for

E 1 I recently started working in the insurance industry.
2 We export automotive parts to companies in other countries.
3 Good to see you again.
4 He works for ForumTech as a researcher.

F 1 pleasure 2 multinational 3 provide 4 department 5 card

Warm up **A** 1 a, e   2 c, d   3 b, f

B I'm having a **1** <u>problem</u> with my computer. It's not **2** <u>connecting</u> to the internet. I think it might be **3** <u>infected</u> with a virus. I tried installing the newest **4** <u>version</u> of the antivirus software, but it didn't work. I think I should call the IT **5** <u>technician</u>.

Quiz 1 B   2 B   3 A   4 C   5 C

Real Communication

1

A	Hi, Janice. How are things with you?
B	Not so great, Kenny. Something is **1** <u>wrong</u> with my computer, I'm afraid.
A	What seems to be the problem?
B	I'm having problems adjusting the language **2** <u>settings</u>.
A	Oh, I see. I had the same problem last week, actually. Maybe I can help.
B	Oh, that would be great, thanks! How did you fix it?
A	Well, first, have you tried **3** <u>rebooting</u> your computer?
B	Yes, I did that straight away, but it's still not working right.
A	OK, in that case you should **4** <u>install</u> the newest **5** <u>version</u> of the operating system.
B	Oh, is that the problem? Ok, I'll try that next. Thanks a lot, Kenny.
A	My pleasure. Let me know if it works!

2

A	Hello, this is Sharon in IT, how can I help you?
B	Hi, Sharon, this is Ray Stevens over in human resources. Can you send an IT **1** <u>technician</u> to the HR department?
A	All of our technicians are busy at the moment. What seems to be the problem?
B	Well, the fax machine is **2** <u>offline</u>. It's rather urgent, I'm afraid.
A	Oh, I see. Maybe we can fix this over the phone. First, try turning the fax machine off and back on again. Sometimes that works.
B	OK, let me try that… No, it's still offline, unfortunately. Maybe the WIFI is **3** <u>down</u>?
A	No, I don't think that's it. The fax machines are not connected to WIFI. Why don't you try reconnecting the **4** <u>cable</u> that plugs into the back of the machine?
B	All right, I'll try that… Still no connection, I'm afraid.
A	OK. Look at the **5** <u>display</u> on the front. Do you see a green light there?
B	No, there's a blinking red light.
A	Oh, I see. We'll need to send the technician in that case. Can you wait until 11:30?
B	Yes, that's no problem. Thanks for your help, Sharon.

A 1 a   2 b   3 b   4 a

B In dialogue 1, Janice is having a problem adjusting the **1** <u>language</u> settings on her computer. Kenny already solved this problem with his computer last week, so he offers to help. He advises Kelly to **2** <u>reboot</u> her computer, but she has already tried that. He tells her to **3** <u>install</u> the newest version of the operating system. Janice will try that solution next.

In dialogue 2, Ray Stevens from the human resources department calls the IT department, and Sharon answers the phone. Ray tells Sharon that he needs an IT **4** <u>technician</u> because the fax machine is **5** <u>offline</u>. Sharon advises Ray to turn the machine off and on again, but it doesn't work. Next, he tries **6** <u>reconnecting</u> the cable, but it also doesn't work. The light on the fax machine is blinking red, so Sharon will send a technician at 11:30.

Practice A Sample Answers

Colleague	Hi, do you need help with something?
You	Hello. **1** I'm not able to receive a fax.
Colleague	Oh, I see. What have you tried so far?
You	I've tried **2** turning it off and back on again.
Colleague	Ok. Did you try reconnecting the cable?
You	Yes, but it still isn't working. **3** Could you send an IT technician to look at it?
Colleague	No problem, we'll send someone over. Is there anything else?
You	**4** Yes, we need more printer paper, too.

Practice B Sample Answers

Colleague	Were you able to solve that internet problem?
You	Yes, it was no big deal. **1** I just reset the router.
Colleague	OK, good. We need it for that conference call later.
You	Yes, I'm glad we didn't need to call the IT technician.
Colleague	By the way, I'm heading to the supply closet. Do you need anything?
You	Yes, actually! **2** Could you get me a box of staples?
Colleague	Sure, I'll grab a box for you. Anything else?
You	**3** We're out of coffee in the break room.
Colleague	All right, I'll ask the office manager about that.
You	Thanks. By the way, **4** the printer is jammed.
Colleague	Oh, really? Maybe I can fix it myself. I'll take a look when I get back.
You	Thanks so much!

Review

A 1 reset 2 jammed 3 convert 4 cable

B 1 a 2 b 3 b

C 1 a 2 c 3 b

D 1 reboot 2 out of 3 technician 4 supply

E 1 I asked the office manager for an ink cartridge.

2 We need more printer paper in the sales department.

3 Have you tried resetting the router?

4 The software is not installing properly.

F 1 printer paper 2 supply closet 3 IT technician 4 rebooting 5 down

Warm up **A** 1 c, e 2 a, b 3 d, f

B It's a large **1** project, so the whole team will be involved. Jose will **2** oversee the sales team, and Andre will be in **3** charge of creating a new advertising approach. I **4** need you to work with Charles to design packaging. It's **5** due next month so we need to get started right away.

Quiz 1 C 2 A 3 B 4 B 5 C

Real Communication

1

A Hi, Chen, how are things?

B Pretty good, Barbara. So, tell me about this new marketing project. Are you **1** overseeing the project timeline?

A Yes, I'm the taskmaster, I suppose. I put James Conway **2** in charge of the market strategy. Do you know James?

B Yes, we worked together on a project last year. I think he's a good choice for that.

A Yeah, I hope so. And Priya is **3** responsible for managing the budget.

B Sounds good to me. Is there anything I can help with?

A Actually, if you've got time, **4** you could meet with James and share ideas. I'm sure he would appreciate the help.

B Sure, I'd be happy to help him get started. When is the deadline?

A It needs to be done by October 15th **5** at the latest.

2

A Hey Raj, Let's set up a meeting for next week and we'll get started on this project.

B Great. What day works best for you, Alexandre?

A Let me check my schedule... I'm totally **1** swamped on Monday... but my schedule is **2** wide open on Tuesday morning.

B Oh, my schedule is a little **3** tight in the mornings. Can we make it Wednesday?

A Yes, Wednesday would be fine. What time works for you?

B I have meetings right after lunch until 3:00, but I'm free after that.

A All right. I usually **4** get off early on Wednesdays to pick up my daughter from school, but if we can meet at 3:30, it will be fine for me.

B Are you sure? I'm sure we can finish by 4:00 or 4:30 at the latest.

A Yes, that's no problem. Is there anything you want me to do before then?

B Well, **5** why don't you do a little research on the competition? I'll prepare a basic project outline for us to discuss.

A Sounds great. See you then!

A 1 b 2 a 3 b 4 a

B In dialogue 1, Chen is asking his colleague about a new **1** marketing project. He learns that James Conway is in charge of market strategy and Priya is **2** responsible for the budget. Chen is asked to meet with James and share ideas. The **3** deadline for the project is October 15th.

In dialogue 2, Raj and Alexandre are trying to arrange a meeting for next week. Monday doesn't work for Alexandre, and Tuesday **4** mornings are not good for Raj, so they decide on **5** Wednesday afternoon. They agree to meet at 3:30. Before the meeting, Alexandre will do some research and Raj will create a **6** project outline.

Practice A Sample Answers

Colleague	Are you almost finished with the budget report?
You	Yes, I will have it done by the end of the day.
Colleague	We need to set up a meeting.
You	1 Which day works best for you?
Colleague	I'm free on Tuesday. Does that work for you?
You	No, sorry. 2 My schedule is a little tight on Tuesday.
Colleague	OK. Is there another day that works better for you?
You	3 My schedule is wide open on Thursday.
Colleague	All right, that works for me, too. Are you free at 3:30?
You	Actually, 4 could we make it 4:00?
Colleague	Yes, that works for me.
You	OK, perfect. 5 I'll see you then. Goodbye.

Practice B Sample Answers

Colleague	What role would you like me to play in the team?
You	1 You'll be in charge of product design.
Colleague	All right, that sounds good to me. Who's in charge of research?
You	2 Kimberly will be responsible for research.
Colleague	I see. What about Joyce?
You	3 Joyce will oversee the budgeting.
Colleague	Great! Is there anything you want me to get started on today?
You	Yes. 4 I need you to create a few basic sketches.

Review

A 1 due   2 charge   3 plate   4 push

B 1 a   2 a   3 b

C 1 b   2 a   3 c

D 1 overseeing   2 overtime   3 and   4 tight

E 1 I'd like you to come in early tomorrow.
2 You'll be in charge of the marketing team.
3 Maybe you could start working on the old documents.
4 The progress report is due next Tuesday.

F 1 come in early   2 deadline   3 latest   4 available   5 make

04 Talking on the Phone

Warm up

A 1 a, d   2 b, e   3 c, f

B Please let her **1** know that Samuel from the Chicago office called **2** regarding her concerns about next month's conference in Singapore. Also, please **3** tell her that I'll be out of the office on Monday and Tuesday, but if she needs to **4** reach me for any reason, she can contact me on my **5** mobile.

Quiz   1 B   2 C   3 B   4 B   5 A

Real Communication

1

A	Good morning, Gosling Medical, how may I direct your call?
B	Hello, could you **1** transfer me to Lucia Ballesteros, please?
A	Sure, let me see if she's in. May I ask who's calling?
B	Yes, this is Jeong-hyun Kim from Fidelity Security.
A	Thank you. **2** Could you hold for just a moment?
B	Yes, that's fine.
A	I'm sorry but it seems that she's out of the office at the moment. Can I **3** take a message?
B	Yes, please. Could you tell her that I'm sorry but I have to cancel lunch tomorrow unfortunately, but I'm available Friday at the same time if she's available.
A	I'm sorry, **4** I didn't quite catch that. Did you say Friday?
B	Yes, that's right. Friday at the same time.
A	Got it. Can you give me a number where she can reach you?
B	Yes, it's 618-2165.
A	Okay, I'll pass on your message. **5** You have a great day.
B	Thank you. Goodbye.

2

A	Janix Piping London, Roya Karim here.
B	Hi Roya, **1** This is Ji-min at the Seoul branch. I'm calling for Vijay in marketing.
A	**2** Could you tell me what it's about?
B	I'm calling about some issues related to next month's conference in Chicago.
A	Ah, okay. If you could hold for just one moment, I'll transfer you to his office.
B	Great. Thanks Roya.
A	… I'm sorry, I'm afraid Vijay is **3** out of the office at the moment.
B	Oh, I see. Do you know when he'll be back?
A	I'm not entirely sure, but probably after lunch. **4** Would you like to leave a message?
B	No message, thank you. Could you just tell him I called?
A	Sure, not a problem. **5** Is there anything else you need help with?
B	No, that's all. Thank you for your help.
A	You're welcome. Goodbye now.
B	Goodbye.

A 1 b   2 a   3 a   4 b

B In dialogue 1, Jeong-hyun is calling **1** Gosling Medical to talk to Lucia. She wants to **2** cancel their lunch appointment for tomorrow and perhaps reschedule for Friday. Lucia isn't in the office, so Jeong-hyun **3** leaves a message for her.

In dialogue 2, Ji-min is looking for 4 <u>information</u> about the conference in Chicago. She calls the 5 <u>London</u> branch of her company and asks to speak to Vijay. He is out of the 6 <u>office</u>, so Ji-min asks Roya to let Vijay know that she called.

Try it Yourself

Practice A Sample Answers

Colleague	Hello, my name is Kendrick Rolly.
You	1 <u>I'm sorry, could you repeat that?</u>
Colleague	Kendrick Rolly. From Rolly Supply.
You	I'm sorry, 2 <u>Could you spell your last name for me?</u>
Colleague	Sure, it's R as in rabbit, O as in octopus, L as in lamp, L as in lamp, Y as in yes.
You	OK, I got it now, thank you. How can I direct your call?
Colleague	I'm calling to speak to Mr. Shay in sales.
You	3 <u>Could I put you on hold while I transfer you?</u>

Practice B Sample Answers

Colleague	Hello, this is David speaking. How can I help you?
You	1 <u>I'm calling to speak to Christian Thomas.</u>
Colleague	OK. Can I have your name, please?
You	2 <u>Yes, this is Jimin Kim.</u>
Colleague	Sorry, could you spell your first name for me?
You	3 <u>Sure, it's J as in jaguar, I as in indigo, M as in mountain, I as in indigo, N as in night.</u>
Colleague	Got it. Could you hold for just a moment while I transfer you?
You	Sure, I'll hold.
Colleague	I'm sorry, Mr. Thomas is on another call. Would you like to hold or leave a message?
You	4 <u>I would like to leave a message, please.</u>
Colleague	All right, what message would you like me to deliver?
You	5 <u>Please tell him that our Monday meeting has been changed to 10:30 am.</u>

Review

A 1 let her know 2 out of 3 speak 4 call me back

B 1 c 2 b 3 a

C 1 b 2 c 3 a

D 1 Would 2 in 3 May 4 leave

E 1 May I speak to Kieran please?
2 I'm sorry, but she's not in right now.
3 Just let her know Heather called.
4 Thanks for calling Wentz Sportswear, how may I help you?

F 1 direct 2 transfer 3 let 4 moment 5 help 6 about

Warm up **A** 1 b, d 2 a, f 3 c, e

B Okay, everyone. Let's get started. I've called this **1** meeting because we need to **2** discuss some problems. I know many of you have strong **3** opinions on these ongoing issues, but I want this meeting to be **4** organized, so please wait for each issue to be **5** introduced before you express your opinion on it.

Quiz 1 B 2 C 3 A 4 C 5 B

Real Communication

1

A	Good morning, everyone. If I could have **1** your attention, we're going to start. I've **2** called this meeting to discuss strategies to increase sales in our southeast market. The first item on the agenda is clarifying why sales have decreased so much. The CEO is getting really frustrated and we need to take action now. Min-jeong, What's your **3** opinion on this?
B	**4** In my opinion, sales have decreased because we simply aren't doing enough market research to find out what the consumer wants. I'm in favor of an aggressive new marketing campaign in every major city in the Southeast. I'm sure the CEO would agree. **5** How do you feel about this?
A	**6** I see your point. I also recently heard our top competitors in the area are outselling us because they have the latest market research. Maybe we need to do the same.

2

A	Okay, let's move on to the next…
B	Amanda, wait, can I just **1** add something to that before we move on? I think it's really important.
A	Sure, **2** go ahead James.
B	Well, I'm not so sure that we should place such a big order just before the holidays. **3** If you look at our numbers for the last few holiday seasons, sales have slumped. Typically, we don't get busy again until late January. We could save some money now if we put in a smaller order.
A	**4** I'm sorry to interrupt, but honestly, I'm **5** not sure I agree with you. Our advertising agency is marketing our product line right now as a Christmas gift idea. I think we could see a huge jump in sales, so we should be ready. Also, if sales aren't very high, it's okay if we have a little extra in stock. We have the space in the warehouse, so it won't be a big problem.

A 1 a 2 a 3 b 4 b

B In dialogue 1, the chair **1** opens the meeting and asks everyone politely for their **2** attention because they are talking amongst themselves. The chair then states the **3** purpose of the meeting, which is the poor **4** sales in their southeast market. He then asks Min-jeong, for her **5** opinion, and she says they need to do more research. He agrees with her.

In dialogue 2, the chair tries to **6** move on to the next point, but he is **7** interrupted by James who wishes to add an opinion. James then expresses his **8** concern over the big order before the holidays. The chair politely interrupts, expresses her disagreement with James's idea, and gives her reasons.

Practice A　Sample Answers

Colleague	Okay, let's quiet down so that we can move on to the next item. Now I'd like to propose finishing our project earlier than scheduled. How do you feel about this?
You	Well, **1** I'm not so sure that's a good idea. We've had problems meeting deadlines in the past.
Colleague	Yes, I suppose you're right. I think the 15th would be a reasonable deadline.
You	**2** I'm not so sure I agree. Maybe we should push it to the 20th.
Colleague	Okay, that's fine. Well, I think we've covered everything, so.....
You	**3** Could I just add something? We still need to go over the sales figures for last quarter.
Colleague	I know that was on the agenda, but we have not received the report from the accounting department yet.
You	Okay, I understand. **4** When will the report be ready?
Colleague	They told me it would be finished by noon today.
You	Got it. I'll stop by their office after lunch and pick it up.

Practice B　Sample Answers

Colleague	I think we've covered everything.
You	**1** If there's nothing else, let's get back to work.
Colleague	Just one more thing, I think it might be better to tell PR first. Plus,...
You	**2** I'm sorry, but we need to move on. We don't have the time to talk about PR issues right now.
Colleague	I understand, we can discuss it later.
You	But before we go, I just want to ask your opinion on the upcoming conference. **3** What are your thoughts?
Colleague	I think the plan looks excellent, but we need to make sure it will fit within our budget.
You	**4** I couldn't agree more. We will ask the project manager for a detailed expense estimate.

Review

A　1 opinion　2 feel　3 think　4 thoughts

B　1 b　2 a　3 c

C　1 b　2 c　3 a

D　1 agree　2 add　3 second　4 point

E　1 Let's go over our conclusions.
　　 2 The purpose of this meeting is to discuss new HR problems.
　　 3 What are your thoughts on the legal issues?
　　 4 Email me if you have any further questions or concerns.

F　1 started　2 called　3 ideas　4 brainstorm　5 agenda　6 opinion

Warm up **A** 1 c, e 2 a, f 3 b, d

B Today, I'd **1** like to talk about some important aspects of sales in the publishing industry. I've **2** divided my presentation into three parts. **3** First, I'll go over the basics of successful sales in the industry. **4** After that, we'll look at how the sales in publishing is changing rapidly. And **5** lastly, I'll discuss the future of the industry.

Quiz 1 C 2 B 3 A 4 C

Real Communication

1

> Good afternoon, everyone. **1** My name is Rick Stevenson, the lead product designer for Amped Stereo. The **2** purpose of my presentation is to familiarize you all with our latest innovations so that you can get a better idea if our systems are right for your businesses. I've **3** divided my presentation into three parts. First, I'll discuss the improvements on our existing products. **4** After that, we'll look at some of our exciting new products. Finally, I'll talk about why our innovations can help your businesses. **5** I only need about ten minutes of your time, and please don't be afraid to interrupt me if you have any questions.

2

> Now, **1** let's move on to our exciting new products. **2** If you'll look at this picture above, you'll see our most powerful speaker yet. **3** A show of hands please. How many of you here are tired of moving around several huge speakers for your big events? Well, now you'll only need one: the Amped SR2000 MegaSound Speaker. I'd just **4** like to highlight that for the price, this speaker will give you triple the sound of your current speakers.

3

> And that **1** concludes my presentation. **2** To recap, we've gone over the latest improvements on our products that you already know and love, our exciting new line of products, and why we're the best for your business. **3** In conclusion, I hope you keep in mind that we have the top-selling audio and stereo products in the country for the last 4 years for a reason, as I've shown you today. **4** Thank you so much for coming. Now, **5** if you have any questions, feel free to ask.

A 1 b 2 a 3 b 4 a

B In the presentation intro, Rick **1** greets his audience and introduces himself. He's presenting his company's **2** innovations to business owners. He **3** outlines his presentation by telling the audience how he's divided the presentation. He **4** instructs the audience to interrupt him if he has any questions.

In the presentation body, Rick talks about the amazing new SR2000 MegaSound Speaker and talks about how powerful it is. In the conclusion, Rick **5** summarizes his three main points. Then, he gives a strong concluding **6** remark for the audience to remember. Finally, he **7** thanks the audience and asks them if they have any **8** questions.

Practice A Sample Answers

1 <u>Hello and welcome everyone.</u> My name is David Kim and I'm s Senior Sales Rep. for Techno Electronics. 2 <u>The purpose of my presentation is</u> to tell you all about our wonderful products. 3 <u>I've divided my presentation into three parts.</u> First, I'll discuss our products' durability and longevity. After that, we'll look at our products' unique features. Finally, we'll go over the great deals we're offering on our latest products. 4 <u>My presentation will be about ten minutes.</u> Please hold any questions for the end of the presentation.

Practice B Sample Answers

1 <u>Finally, that brings us to our great deals.</u> We offer fantastic deals on PCs for your office no matter what your needs. 2 <u>As you can see in this chart</u>, we offer almost 30% discounts for orders of 500 or more units. Also, 3 <u>I just want to emphasize that</u> all of the installation is free and done by our expert tech guys.

4 <u>And that brings me to the end of my presentation.</u> To recap, our products are the most durable, have the newest features, and will save you money. In conclusion, I hope you keep in mind how much Techno products can help your company in the future. Thank you so much for your attention. Now, if you have any questions, feel free to ask.

Review

A 1 for coming   2 emphasize   3 concludes   4 attention

B 1 c   2 a   3 c

C 1 b   2 a   3 c

D 1 see   2 talk   3 free   4 stress

E 1 Welcome everyone and thank for coming.
2 I'd be happy to take a few questions now.
3 I've divided my presentation into three parts.
4 Today I'm here to discuss my company's latest products.

F 1 everything   2 To recap   3 To conclude   4 You've been   5 questions

Warm up **A** 1 a, f 2 b, d 3 c, e

B These jeans come **1** in three different styles, and they are made **2** of high-quality materials. They are very **3** durable , so they last a long time. And the design is **4** practical , so they are perfect for everyday use. We offer them in two **5** colors – blue and black.

Quiz 1 C 2 A 3 A 4 C 5 B

Real Communication

1

A	Lucas, how's it going?
B	Hi Alice, I'm doing well. We just got the **1** sales figures on that new bicycle helmet we released a few months ago, and they're better than we anticipated.
A	Oh that's good! Which helmet are you talking about? The red and green one?
B	Actually, it comes in **2** a variety of colors and patterns. But the black and white model has been our best seller.
A	Oh, I see. So how is this new helmet different from the standard model?
B	Well, it's more **3** durable, for a start. It's practically indestructible. It's made from extremely high-quality materials.
A	I'm glad it's selling so well. The marketing team must be doing a good job.
B	Yes, even with a relatively small **4** advertising budget they've done quite well.
A	How did they do it?
B	They launched a really impressive social media **5** campaign. We've managed to get a few influencers to do video reviews, and that helped a lot.
A	Sounds great. I should suggest that to my team as well.
B	Yes, I totally recommend it.

2

A	Excuse me, would you like some help?
B	Actually, I'm just browsing.
A	OK, well let me know if you have any questions.
B	Actually, I was looking at this dress. Does it **1** come in any other sizes?
A	Yes, that's the 2 there, but we also have it in a 4 and a 6.
B	OK, I think I'll try on the 4 if that's all right.
A	Of course, no problem. I love that dress, actually. I have one at home myself. It's so **2** versatile, you can wear it anywhere.
B	Is it 100% cotton?
A	Actually, it's **3** made of an 80% cotton blended fabric. It actually helps to prevent wrinkles, and it breathes really well.
B	Oh, looking at the price, I'm afraid it's a little expensive for me.
A	Well, we're offering a **4** 15% discount on all dresses until the end of the week. You should also consider joining our membership program for an extra 5% discount.
B	Do I need to pay anything to join?
A	No, it's totally free. You'll get **5** exclusive discounts on our online store as well.
B	All right, well, thanks for the information. Where can I find the fitting room?

A 1 b 2 a 3 b 4 a

B In dialogue 1, Lucas tells Alice about the success of their new **1** bicycle helmet. It comes in a **2** variety of colors and patterns, and it is very durable. The marketing team had a small budget, but their **3** social media campaign was very successful.

In dialogue 2, a customer asks a store attendant about a dress. The dress 4 <u>comes in</u> three sizes, and it is made of an 80% cotton blend. The 5 <u>price</u> is a little high, but there is a 15% discount on all dresses in the store. The customer can get an additional 6 <u>5% discount</u> by joining their membership program.

Try it Yourself

Practice A Sample Answers

| Colleague | How is the marketing campaign for the new car going? |
| You | It's going well. 1 <u>The sales forecast is very promising.</u> |

| Colleague | How about the digital marketing? |
| You | 2 <u>Our social media pages are getting a lot more engagement.</u> |

| Colleague | That's great news. What do you think is the cause? |
| You | Well, our SEO specialist is doing really good work. |

| Colleague | So what is our target market? |
| You | 3 <u>We are targeting young adults, men in particular.</u> |

| Colleague | Great. What is the main feature we are promoting? |
| You | 4 <u>The main feature is that it is extremely user-friendly.</u> |

| Colleague | Excellent. Are you having any difficulties? |
| You | Actually, 5 <u>our advertising budget is a little small.</u> |

Practice B Sample Answers

| Colleague | Are you the new social media marketer? |
| You | Yes, right. 1 <u>My name is Jimin Kang. It's a pleasure to meet you.</u> |

| Colleague | Nice to meet you, too. I'm Chad Stevens. So what are you working on? |
| You | 2 <u>Right now I'm designing a new banner ad.</u> |

| Colleague | I see. Have you noticed any problem with our marketing efforts? |
| You | 3 <u>Well, the conversion rates on our video ad are way too low.</u> |

| Colleague | Oh, I didn't realize that. Well, let me know if you need anything. |
| You | 4 <u>Thanks Chad. See you later.</u> |

Review

A 1 guarantee   2 trending   3 sales figures   4 target

B 1 b   2 a   3 b

C 1 c   2 b   3 a

D 1 research   2 target   3 generating   4 price

E 1 Our new phone is incredibly user-friendly.
2 This sweater is our best-selling item.
3 I am disappointed by last month's sales figures.
4 We need a bigger advertising budget.

F 1 made of   2 durable   3 versatile   4 ended   5 Guarantee

Warm up **A** 1 b, e 2 a, f 3 c, d

B Hello, I would like to **1** place an order for 250 boxes of drinking straws. The **2** delivery date is very important, as we need them within 15 days. I saw the **3** price list on your website, but I was wondering if you **4** offer a **5** discount for ordering in bulk. Thank you for your prompt attention.

Quiz 1 C 2 A 3 C 4 C 5 C

Real Communication

1

A	Good afternoon, Skiles Inc. How can I help you?
B	Hello, this is Jamie Adams calling from Harber-Corwin. We're **1** interested in purchasing some picture frames.
A	Sure, I can help you with that. How many would you like to order?
B	**2** We're going to need 75 units.
A	Actually, we have an **3** order minimum of 100 units.
B	All right, 100 units should be no problem. Could we have a price estimate?
A	You can find our price list on our website, but I can send you a **4** price estimate by the end of the day.
B	Great. Do you ship internationally? We're located in Alberta, Canada.
A	Yes, we ship to Canada. The delivery will take approximately two to three weeks.
B	Perfect. How can I proceed with the order?
A	I'll email you an **5** order form to fill out. As soon as we process your order, we'll send you an invoice with instructions for payment. Can I have your email address, please?
B	Sure, it's jamie_adams@harbercorwin.net.

2

A	Hello, is this Goodwin Supply?
B	Yes, it is. My name is Alice. How can I help you?
A	This is Todd calling from Perfect Grill. I'm calling **1** in reference to our order number 52319.
B	OK, let me pull that up on my computer... Yes, here it is. Unfortunately, it looks like one of the products you ordered is no longer in stock.
A	Yes, we never received the ceramic mugs we ordered. I saw in your **2** catalog that item number 529 is quite similar. How many of those do you have in stock?
B	Our warehouse is fully stocked with that item. How many would you like to purchase?
A	Could you send 150 units **3** as soon as possible?
B	Yes, not a problem. We can offer you the **4** wholesale price, which includes a 5% discount.
A	Great. Could we also have 50 units of item #399?
B	The long-stem wine glasses? Certainly. I'll add that to your order. Is there anything else?
A	No, that's everything. When can we expect to receive the **5** shipment?
B	As soon as the invoice is paid, we'll process your order and ship it out the same day. Your order will arrive within five business days.
A	Great, thank you very much. Could you send the invoice by fax, please?
B	Certainly. We have your fax number on file here.

A 1 b 2 a 3 a 4 b

B In dialogue 1, Jamie Adams calls the supplier to **1** place an order for picture frames. She wants to order 75 units, but there is an **2** order minimum of 100 units. She will receive a **3** price estimate by the end of the day, and the shipment will arrive in Alberta in two or three weeks.

In dialogue 2, Todd from Mountainview Grill calls the supplier about an order. He did not receive the ceramic mugs he ordered, as they are out of 4 stock. He orders a similar product instead and receives a discount for buying in 5 bulk. He also adds an order for wine glasses. The delivery will arrive within 5 days, and the 6 invoice will be sent by fax.

Try it Yourself

Practice A Sample Answers

Colleague	I would like to place an order for 30 boxes of ballpoint pens.
You	1 Unfortunately, we have an order minimum of 50 boxes.
Colleague	All right, 50 boxes then. We're also going to need some staples.
You	2 How many are you going to need?
Colleague	50 boxes of staples, as well.
You	No problem. 3 Do you have any other questions?
Colleague	How do I proceed with payment?
You	4 I will send you an invoice by email with instructions for payment.

Practice B Sample Answers

Colleague	Hello, can I help you?
You	Yes, 1 I'd like to place a purchase order.
Colleague	What would you like to order?
You	2 Could you send 200 units of item number 291?
Colleague	All right, I've added that to your order. Is there anything else?
You	3 Could we have a price estimate for that?
Colleague	The final price will be listed in your invoice.
You	4 Do you ship internationally?
Colleague	Which country are you located in?
You	Our company is located in Germany.
Colleague	I will include a delivery quote in your invoice.
You	5 Thank you very much. Have a nice day.

Review

A   1 reference   2 update   3 shipped   4 confirm

B   1 b   2 a   3 c

C   1 a   2 b   3 c

D   1 out   2 place   3 list   4 confirm

E   1 Could you send 75 units as soon as possible?
2 There is a discount for buying in bulk.
3 I'm calling in reference to order number 1029.
4 How many books do you have in stock?

F   1 catalog   2 stock   3 wholesale   4 internationally   5 Estimate

Warm up **A** 1 c, e 2 a, f 3 b, d

B On the whole, your **1** proposal is reasonable. I don't see any **2** problem with the duration of the contract, and I'm happy **3** with the vacation time and benefits. However, I have some **4** reservations about the salary. If you can be **5** flexible on this point, I would be willing to accept the offer.

Quiz 1 C 2 A 3 A 4 C 5 C

Real Communication

1

A	So Mr. Martinez, have you had time to review the job offer we sent you?
B	I have, yes. I hope that we can discuss a few points.
A	Sure, of course. What would you like to talk about?
B	I have some **1** reservations about the benefits package. I didn't see anything about a pension program.
A	Oh, that's mentioned briefly on page three. Your contract includes a full **2** benefits package, including enrollment in our pension program.
B	All right, great. Would you consider increasing the base salary?
A	I'm sorry, this is our **3** best offer. You will, however, be eligible for a salary increase after 6 months, depending on your performance.
B	I see. In exchange for a lower salary, would you agree to a higher overtime rate?
A	That sounds like a **4** fair suggestion. I will discuss it with the director.
B	All right. I'm happy with everything else.
A	If we can increase the overtime rate, would you be willing to sign a contract later this week?
B	Yes, I think I'm ready to **5** move forward.

2

A	Thank you for coming. Mr. Sanders, we are **1** prepared to offer your company this proposal. Please take a few minutes to review it.
B	OK, thank you, Ms. White... I notice here that the contract would be valid for only six months. At that point, the prices could be increased, is that right?
A	Well, that's true, yes. Six months is our standard contract duration with a relatively new company such as yours.
B	From my **2** perspective, that puts us in an unstable position. I would prefer a longer contract. Would you consider extending it to two years?
A	I'm afraid that's out of the question. We might be willing to **3** compromise on the price, but the contract duration is non-negotiable.
B	Well, it's a shame we can't agree on this point. We may have to look elsewhere.
A	Let's see if we can find some **4** common ground. In exchange for extending your contract to one year, would you allow us to add some conditions? If the conditions are not met after six months, the contract will expire.
B	Well, let me **5** sleep on it. I would need to see the specifics on these conditions you mentioned.
A	Yes, I understand. I'll have a revised contract drafted and sent to your office by the end of the week.
B	Thank you. I'll be in touch.

A 1 a 2 b 3 b 4 b

B In dialogue 1, Mr. Martinez discusses a job offer with a recruiter. He has a question about the pension program, and the recruiter explains that the contract includes a full benefits **1** package. The recruiter **2** refuses to adjust the salary but considers increasing the **3** overtime rate.

In dialogue 2, Mr. Sanders discusses a contract offered to his company by Ms. White. Mr. Sanders would like the **4** duration of the contract to be increased from six months to two years. After some **5** negotiating, Ms. White agrees to extend to the contract, but insists on adding some **6** conditions to the contract.

Try it Yourself

Practice A Sample Answers

Colleague	Are you ready to sign the contract?
You	Actually, **1** I have some reservations about the salary.
Colleague	From our perspective, this salary is suitable for your level of experience.
You	**2** I take your point; however, would you consider increasing the salary?
Colleague	What salary do you feel would be appropriate?
You	I would like the salary to be 20% higher than stated in this contract.
Colleague	We may be able to increase the salary by 5%.
You	**3** I could accept a 15% increase.
Colleague	I'll see what I can do. What about the benefits package?
You	**4** I'm happy with that.
Colleague	If we can increase the salary by 10%, would you be willing to sign?
You	**5** Possibly. I'd like to stop and think about it for a little while.

Practice B Sample Answers

Client	I read your proposal, and I think it is quite reasonable.
You	Great! **1** Would you be willing to sign a contract right now?
Client	Well, I have just one reservation. We would like deliveries twice a month instead of once a month.
You	**2** I don't see any problem with that. However, we would need to raise the price.
Client	That seems a bit unreasonable. Would you consider delivering every 3 weeks?
You	**3** That's a fair suggestion.
Client	I'm glad we've found some common ground.
You	**4** Would you be willing to sign a contract today?

Review

A **1** terms **2** flexible **3** unreasonable **4** prepared

B **1** b **2** c **3** a

C **1** b **2** a **3** c

D **1** willing **2** to **3** perspective **4** package

E **1** I'm afraid we can't agree on the delivery fee.
2 I'm afraid that's out of the question.
3 I'm willing to compromise on the vacation time.
4 I think we're ready to move forward.

F **1** reservations **2** consider **3** perspective **4** compromise **5** terms

10 Money Matters

A 1 b, c   2 e, f   3 a, d

B As you can see here, overall sales jumped **1** by ten percent between November **2** and December. Sales of women's clothing, in particular, rose **3** from $40,000 **4** to $45,000, and this number is expected to reach $50,000 by the end of the year.

Quiz   1 B   2 A   3 C   4 C   5 A

Real Communication

1

A	Hi, Fernanda. How was your meeting with the director?
B	Hello, Chad. It went really well. She's very happy with our progress this quarter.
A	Yeah? What did she say?
B	She said our department is one of the most **1** successful in the company.
A	Oh, that's great. Did you show her our **2** sales forecast for next month? I think it's really promising.
B	I did, yes. She is a little worried about our expenses, however, as they've risen significantly over the last several months.
A	That's true. But they should **3** level off this quarter.
B	I hope so. If we want to stay competitive, we need to maintain our **4** profit margin.
A	Agreed. Did you explain our cash flow issue? If we had more **5** cash on hand, we could place bigger orders and save some money on materials.
B	She said she would work on it. We need to clear some of our debt first.
A	That makes sense. In any case, I'm glad she's noticed how successful we've been.
B	Agreed. Things are really looking up!

2

A	Felix, could you present the quarterly sales report for the publishing department, please?
B	Yes, I would be happy to. If you'll take a look at the graph here, you'll see that we're experiencing a **1** decline in textbook sales.
A	How is it, then, that profits have remained steady?
B	Well, sales of children's books have risen by 20%, so we've been able to stay **2** profitable.
A	I see. Is there a reason that textbook sales have been so weak?
B	The textbook industry as a whole is experiencing a recession. Students are moving toward ebooks and textbook rentals. We have also shifted a lot of our marketing budget to other areas, mainly literature and self-help books.
A	I see. Textbooks are so costly to produce, we can't really afford to **3** take a loss on them. Is there any way to reduce expenses?
B	We are looking at ways to improve the **4** profit margin to compensate for the drop in sales.
A	I'd like to hear some of those ideas. We'll meet next week to talk about that. What is the forecast for next quarter?
B	We expect to see a **5** rise in profits, especially as the holiday season approaches.
A	Excellent. Thank you, Felix.
B	My pleasure.

A 1 b   2 b   3 a   4 a

B In dialogue 1, Chad asks Fernanda about her meeting with the director. The director is satisfied with their sales **1** forecast, but she is worried about their **2** expenses. Chad asks about the cash flow issue, and the director said she would work on it, but the current level of **3** debt is a problem.

In dialogue 2, Felix presents the sales report to his manager. He explains that textbooks sales have declined, but **4** profits are strong because of the success of children's books. Felix explains why **5** textbook sales have been weak, and he promises to find ways to **6** reduce expenses. He expects profits to go up next quarter.

Try it Yourself

Practice A Sample Answers

Colleague	Congratulations on the success of your new company!
You	Thank you! However, **1** we are still not profitable yet.
Colleague	That's common for a new business. How are your sales?
You	**2** Last month our sales rose by 15%.
Colleague	Oh, good! Any predictions for next quarter?
You	Well, **3** there will likely be a steady rise in revenue.
Colleague	That's great to hear. Are you struggling with anything?
You	**4** Our overhead is a little high, so we're trying to cut expenses.

Practice B Sample Answers

Colleague	Tell me what happened from January to March.
You	**1** Sales jumped from 20,000 to 35,000.
Colleague	OK, and what happened in the second quarter?
You	**2** There was a sharp decline in sales.
Colleague	Can you describe the sales figures in the third quarter?
You	**3** Sales fluctuated between 15 and 22 thousand.
Colleague	And how about during the final quarter of the year?
You	**4** Sales remained steady at around 20,000.

Review

A 1 assets   2 promising   3 thrifty   4 overhead

B 1 b   2 b   3 c

C 1 c   2 b   3 a

D 1 recession   2 overhead   3 off   4 profitable

E 1 We are trying to avoid going bankrupt.
2 This is one of our most lucrative projects.
3 Profits have risen by 10% this year.
4 We can improve our profit margin by cutting expenses.

F 1 dropped   2 jumped   3 fluctuate   4 cash on hand   5 overhead

Warm up **A** 1 c, e   2 b, d   3 a, f

B Thank you for 1 <u>bringing</u> this to our attention. I understand this is frustrating for you, and we 2 <u>take</u> full responsibility 3 <u>for</u> the problem. It appears there was a misunderstanding with our production facility. We would like to offer you a 4 <u>full</u> refund, and we ask that you please 5 <u>submit</u> a formal complaint through our website.

Quiz 1 A   2 C   3 C   4 B   5 A

Real Communication

1

A	Hello, how can I help you today?
B	Hi. I'm calling to make a 1 <u>complaint</u>.
A	Oh, what seems to be the problem?
B	I bought a pair of boots from your online shop, and the actual product did not match the description on the website.
A	Thank you for bringing this to 2 <u>our attention</u>. Can you tell me which boots you purchased?
B	The knee-high work boots. I ordered the dark brown, and the boots I received are much lighter than I expected.
A	I'm very sorry to hear that. Can you give me your order number?
B	It's 51399.
A	OK, it appears there was some kind of 3 <u>mix-up</u> with our distributer. We would like to offer you 4 <u>an in-store exchange</u> for that item. We will send you a shipping label, so you can send them back.
B	That seems like a lot of work on my part. This is extremely frustrating!
A	You have 5 <u>every reason</u> to be upset. We take full responsibility for the mistake, and we would like to offer you a 25% discount on your next purchase by way of apology.
B	Well, thank you for your help.
A	Thank you for calling. I hope you have a nice day.

2

A	Hello, JC Supply, this is Sheila speaking. How can I help you?
B	Hello, this is Pedro Romano from Bradley Meyers. 1 <u>I'm afraid</u> there is a problem with the fax machines we received.
A	I'm very sorry to 2 <u>hear that</u>. What seems to be the problem?
B	They are simply not turning on. We plug them in and nothing happens.
A	I see. I'm sorry to hear that the items are 3 <u>defective</u>. I'll arrange for a technician to visit your office and investigate the problem.
B	Well, I called last week and was promised the same thing.
A	Let me open your account here, just a moment… OK, it looks like there was some 4 <u>miscommunication</u> with the technician. I'm very sorry about that.
B	This is really causing problems for us. We already got rid of our old machines.
A	I completely understand where you're 5 <u>coming from</u>. I am contacting the technician right now, and he will be there by the end of the day.
B	Thank you for taking care of this.
A	You're very welcome.

A 1 b   2 a   3 a   4 a

B In dialogue 1, a customer is calling to **1** complain about some boots that he ordered online. The **2** color of the boots did not match the online description. The customer service representative explains the process of exchanging the boots. The customer is upset, and the customer service representative **3** offers a 25% discount.

In dialogue 2, Pedro Romano calls an office supply company to explain that the new **4** fax machines he ordered are not working. Sheila apologizes, explains that there was some miscommunication with the **5** technician, and **6** promises that the technician will arrive today.

Try it Yourself

Practice A Sample Answers

Supplier	How can I help you?
You	Hello. **1** I would like to make a complaint.
Supplier	What seems to be the problem?
You	**2** The items I ordered were never delivered.
Supplier	Can you tell me your order number, please?
You	Yes, the order number is 59910.
Supplier	Oh, it appears there was some kind of mix-up with the delivery service.
You	**3** What are you going to do to fix this problem?
Supplier	We can offer you an in-store exchange or a full refund.
You	**4** I'd like to receive a full refund on my order.
Supplier	Yes, we'll process your refund right away.
You	**5** Thank you for your help. Goodbye.

Practice B Sample Answers

Customer	I'm calling to make a complaint.
You	**1** What seems to be the problem?
Customer	The phone I received is not working properly.
You	**2** I sincerely apologize for the inconvenience.
Customer	I read positive reviews about it, so I'm very disappointed.
You	**3** I completely understand where you're coming from.
Customer	Can you give me a refund?
You	**4** We can offer you an in-story exchange, and we'd like to offer you a 20% discount on your next purchase.

Review

A   1 reason   2 apologize   3 attention   4 disappointed   **F**   1 complain   2 seems   3 sincerest   4 upset   5 complaint

B   1 c   2 b   3 b

C   1 c   2 a   3 b

D   1 apologize   2 defective   3 responsibility   4 where

E   1 You can submit a formal complaint on our website.

2 I'm disappointed with the service I received.

3 We would like to offer you a discount on your next purchase.

4 You have every reason to be upset.

Warm up **A** 1 c, d   2 b, e   3 a, f

B 1 <u>Hello</u> Jacob,

2 <u>Thank</u> you for your quick response to the urgent memo. I think Sofia has found a solution to the 3 <u>problem</u> with the Havertown account. We'll process the order again and give them a 25% 4 <u>discount</u> to make them happy. In the meantime, I was hoping you could make sure the other orders that went out this week went smoothly. Please let me 5 <u>know</u> ASAP.

Thanks.

Beverly

Quiz   1 C   2 A

Real Communication

1

1 <u>Dear</u> Kofi Banta,

Thank you so much for getting 2 <u>back to me</u> regarding your company's new R&D report. Your information was quite useful. I'm 3 <u>emailing</u> you now to let you know that our company is very interested in a joint venture after much consideration. 4 <u>We would like to invite</u> you and your team to our office here in Los Angeles early next month to discuss the details in person. We'd love to cover your flight and accommodation as well.

5 <u>Thank you</u> very much again for your excellent report. 6 <u>I look forward to</u> hearing from you very soon.

Thank you,

Marsha Brady

2

1 <u>Hey</u> Amanda,

I hope 2 <u>all is well</u>. Just 3 <u>to let you know</u>, we have a visit from the CEO coming next month. Linda told me that we need to start prepping a bunch of things. Oh, and about the TPS reports, 4 <u>make sure</u> you get them to Mike before the end of the day.

I'll get back to you soon about the preparations for the CEO visit.

5 <u>See you</u>,

Courtney

3

1 <u>Hi</u> Courtney,

Okay. 2 <u>That sounds fine</u>. I think we can have all of that ready before he gets here. And don't worry, I just sent my TPS reports this morning.

Thanks,

Amanda

A   1 a   2 b   3 b   4 a

B   In email 1, Marsha writes to Kofi to express her gratitude for the 1 <u>R&D</u> report. She's so happy about the report that she wants to 2 <u>invite</u> members of Kofi's company to 3 <u>come</u> to L.A. to discuss a possible 4 <u>joint venture</u>.

In emails 2 and 3, Courtney informs Amanda of the CEO's 5 <u>visit</u> next month and reminds her to 6 <u>submit</u> the TPS reports to Mike today. She'll tell Amanda more about the visit later. Amanda responds by telling her that she agrees about the preparations and that she's already turned in the TPS reports.

Practice A Sample Answers

1 Dear Mr. Jenkins,

2 I'm emailing you regarding next month's conference. 3 I wanted to inform you the schedule will be very demanding, so I thought I'd give you an overview.

There will be small presentations all morning from 8 a.m. to 12 p.m. The conference will then give a buffet lunch in the main hall. After that, participants will attend various workshops between 1 p.m. and 3 p.m. You, Mr. Jenkins, will of course be our plenary speaker, so you will give the final speech in the main hall at 3 p.m. sharp.

4 Thank you again very much volunteering your time as a speaker. If you have any questions, 5 feel free to ask. I will let you know if there are changes to the schedule.

Best wishes,

Michael Johnson

Practice B Sample Answers

1 Hey Biff,

2 How are things? Just to let you know, we have an emergency meeting at 4 p.m. today. There's been another issue with the Sao Paolo account. They said that they were billed too much again, so we need to fix problems with accounting.

3 I'm glad that you're back from paternity leave so that you can fix these problems. 4 Let me know if you have any questions.

5 Cheers,

Marty

Review

A 1 reply   2 inform   3 things   4 appreciate

B 1 b   2 a   3 c

C 1 b   2 c   3 a

D 1 understanding   2 hope   3 look   4 for

E 1 I'm writing to let you know that the conference is on the 31st.
2 Thanks for your quick reply to my email.
3 If you have any questions, feel free to ask.
4 I will let you know tomorrow what time the meeting will be.

F 1 reply   2 appreciate   3 inform   4 again   5 let you know